AA
GLOVI
SP/
PORTUGAL

contents

Map pages	ii
Map symbols	iii
Route planner	iv
Distance chart	I
Road atlas	**2-45**
Index and city environs plans	**46-60**

Barcelona	47	Porto	55
Lisboa	52	San Sebastián	57
Madrid	53	Sevilla	58

1st edition February 1996

© The Automobile Association 1996

All rights reserved. No part of this publication may be reproduced, stored in a retrieval system, or transmitted in any form or by any means - electronic, mechanical, photocopying, recording or otherwise, unless the permission of the publisher has been obtained beforehand.

Published by AA Publishing (a trading name of Automobile Association Developments Limited, whose registered office is Norfolk House, Priestley Road, Basingstoke, Hampshire, RG24 9NY. Registered number 1878835).

Mapping produced by the Cartographic Department of The Automobile Association. This atlas has been compiled and produced from the Automaps database utilising electronic and computer technology.

ISBN 0 7495 1189 3

A CIP catalogue for this book is available from the British Library.

Printed in Great Britain by BPC Waterlow Ltd, Dunstable.

The contents of this atlas are believed correct at the time of printing. Nevertheless, the publishers cannot accept any responsibility for errors or omissions or for changes in the details given. They would welcome information to help keep this atlas up to date, please write to the Cartographic Editor, Publishing Division, The Automobile Association, Norfolk House, Priestley Road, Basingstoke, Hampshire, RG24 9NY.

map pages

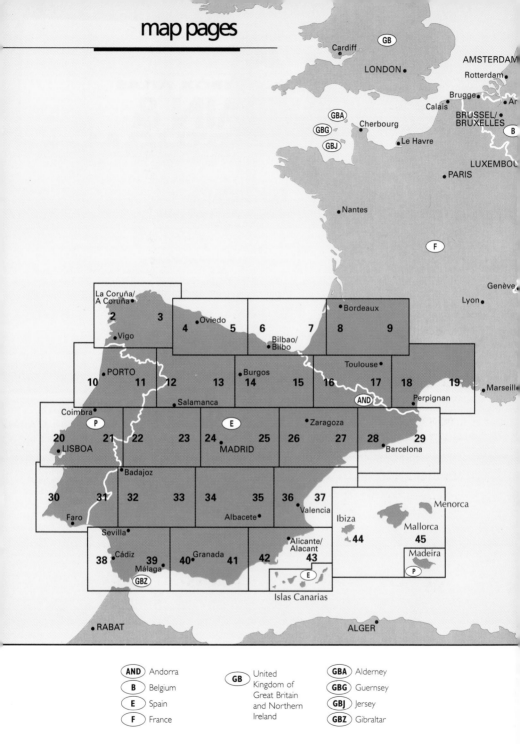

AND	Andorra	
B	Belgium	
E	Spain	
F	France	
GB	United Kingdom of Great Britain and Northern Ireland	
GBA	Alderney	
GBG	Guernsey	
GBJ	Jersey	
GBZ	Gibraltar	

map symbols

Toll motorways

| A55 E55 | Dual carriageway with road numbers |
| Single carriageway |
| Interchange |
| Restricted interchange |
| Service area |
| Under construction |

Non-toll motorways

| A55 E55 | Dual carriageway with road numbers |
| Single carriageway |
| Interchange |
| Restricted interchange |
| Service area |
| Under construction |

National roads

| SS45 | Dual carriageway with road number |
| Single carriageway |

Regional roads

| SS45 | Dual carriageway with road number |
| Single carriageway |

Local roads

| SS453 | Dual carriageway with road number |
| Single carriageway |

| D28 | Minor road with road number |

| 38 | Page overlap and number |

Symbols

E55   E55   European international network numbers

Motorway in tunnel

Road in tunnel

Road under construction

Toll point

24   Distances in kilometres

>>   Gradient 14% and over

>   Gradient 6%-13%

10-6
Furkapass   Mountain pass with closure period
2431

628
PUERTO DE ANGER   Spot height (metres)

Ferry route (all year)

Hovercraft (all year)

Airport (International)

Car transporter (rail)

Mountain railway

Viewpoint (180° or 360°)

Urban area

Town location

Canal

Wooded area

Boundaries

International

National

Unrecognised international

Restricted frontier crossing

scale

1:1 000 000   10 kilometres : 1 centimetre

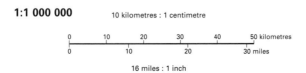

16 miles : 1 inch

iii

Ciudad Real - San Sebastián/Donostia = 685km

685

Cities (E = España, P = Portugal, F = France, AND = Andorra, GBZ = Gibraltar):

- Albacete (E)
- Alicante/Alacant (AND)
- Andorra la Vella (AND)
- Badajoz (E)
- Barcelona (E)
- Bilbao/Bilbo (E)
- Bordeaux (F)
- Burgos (E)
- Cádiz (E)
- Ciudad Real (E)
- Coimbra (P)
- Córdoba (E)
- Cuenca (E)
- Faro (P)
- Gibraltar (GBZ)
- Granada (E)
- La Coruña/A Coruña (E)
- Lagos (P)
- León (E)
- Lisboa (P)
- Madrid (E)
- Málaga (E)
- Mérida (E)
- Murcia (E)
- Nantes (F)
- Oviedo (E)
- Pamplona/Iruñea (E)
- Paris (F)
- Perpignan (F)
- Porto (P)
- Salamanca (E)
- San Sebastián/Donostia (E)
- Santander (E)
- Sevilla (E)
- Toledo (E)
- Toulouse (F)
- Valencia (E)
- Valladolid (E)
- Vigo (E)
- Zaragoza (E)

l

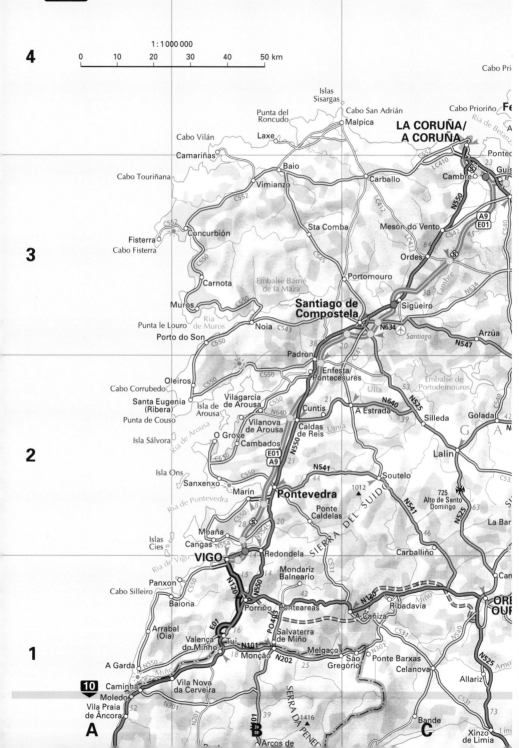

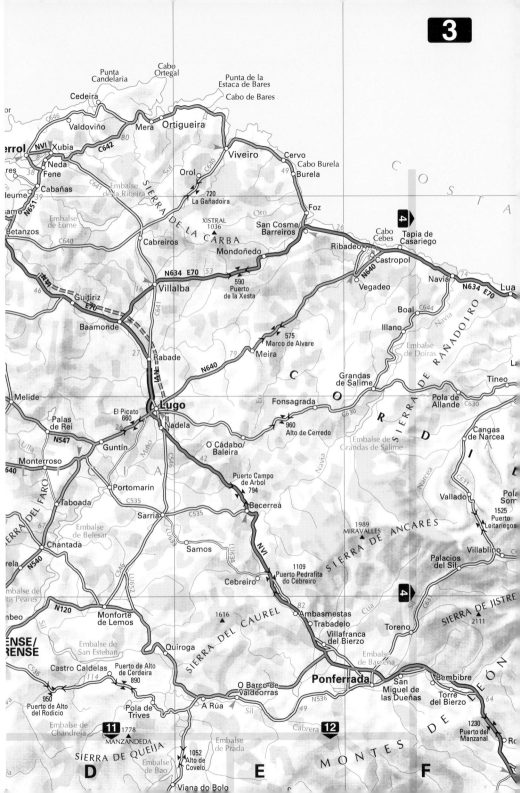

Punta
Candelaria
Cabo
Ortegal
Cedeira
Punta de la
Estaca de Bares
Cabo de Bares
C646
Valdoviño
Mera
Ortigueira
Viveiro
Cervo
Cabo Burela
Burela
Orol
C640
49
Sor
80
errol
NVI
Xubia
C642
Neda
Fene
C641
Embalse
de la Ribeira
720
La Gañadoira
Foz
Cabañas
N651
8
38
39
leume
Embalse
de Eume
Betanzos
C640
Cabreiros
XISTRAL
1036
SIERRA DE LA CARBA
Mondoñedo
San Cosme/
Barreiros
Cabo
Cebes
Tapia de
Casariego
26
4
Ribadeo
Castropol
N640
Navia
74
N634 E70
Lua
N634 E70
53
Villalba
590
Puerto
de la Xesta
Vegadeo
Boal
C644
16
C641
E70
Guitiriz
Baamonde
575
Marco de Alvare
Meira
79
Illano
Navia
Embalse
de Doiras
Rabade
27
N640
C O
R D
I L
Melide
El Picato
660
Lugo
Nadela
Fonsagrada
Grandas
de Salime
Pola de
Allande
C630
Tineo
Palas
de Rei
N547
26
Guntín
O Cádabo/
Baleira
960
Alto de Cerredo
C630
Embalse de
Grandas de Salime
Cangas
de Narcea
Monterroso
C640
Portomarín
C535
42
Puerto Campo
de Arbol
794
Becerreá
Navia
Narcea
C631
Vallado
Pola
Som
1525
Puerto
Leitariegos
Taboada
Sarria
C535
LU633
Samos
1989
MIRAVALLES
SIERRA DE ANCARES
Villablino
SIERRA DEL FARO
67
Chantada
N540
Embalse
de Belesar
LU634
NVI
1109
Puerto Pedrafita
do Cebreiro
Palacios
del Sil
rela
N120
Monforte
de Lemos
Cebreiro
1616
Ambasmestas
Trabadelo
Villafranca
del Bierzo
82
Cua
4
Toreno
SIERRA DE JISTRE
2111
C631
nbeo
Embalse de
os Peares
Embalse de
San Esteban
Quiroga
SIERRA DEL CAUREL
Embalse
de Bárcena
Castro Caldelas
Puerto de Alto
de Cerdeira
890
114
O Barco de
Valdeorras
Ponferrada
San
Miguel de
las Dueñas
Bembibre
Torre
del Bierzo
64
ENSE/
RENSE
C536
950
Puerto de Alto
del Rodicio
Pola de
Trives
A Rúa
Sil
N536
49
1230
Puerto del
Manzanal
Ro
va
Embalse de
Chandreja
11
1778
MANZANEDA
1052
Alto de
Covelo
Embalse
de Prada
Cabrera
12
MONTES DE LEON
SIERRA DE QUEIJA
Embalse
de Bao
Viana do Bolo
D
E
F

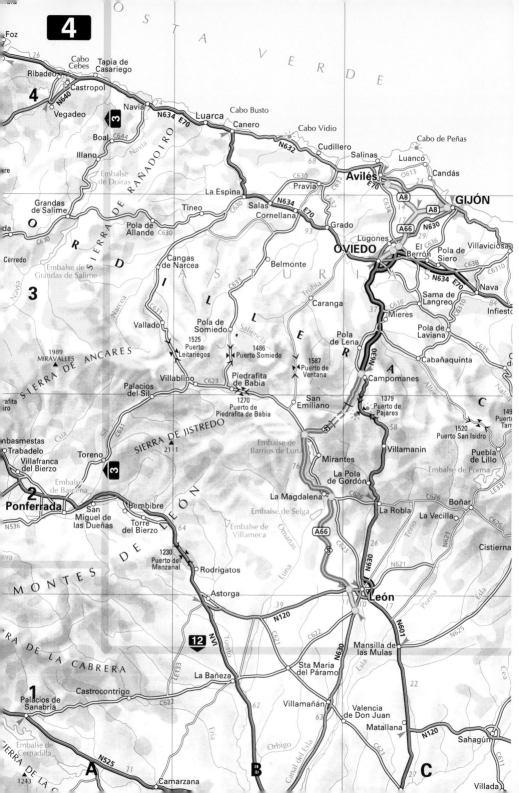

1 : 1 000 000

0   10   20   30   40   50 km

9

Punta de Tazones

Puerto
Lastres

N632

Colunga   La Isla   Punta de
Carreros

Ribadesella

Arriondas

Cangas
de Onis   N634   Cabo Prieto
E70   Llanes

SIERRA DE CUERA

Campo
de Caso

C6312

Arenas   C6312   Unquera   San Vincente
de la Barquera

Covadonga   Cares   Panes   Comillas

Punta del
Dichoso   Santillana
del Mar   Suances   Cabo
Mayor   SANTANDE

Galiza

PICOS DE EUROPA   La Hermida   N634   Cabezón
de la Sal   E70
A67

Oseja de
Sajambre   Embalse del
Palombera   C6374   Las Caldas
de Besaya   N611   Torrelavega   N634   Solares

N   2648   38   C625   N634

1290   FUENTE DE   Puente Viesgo   N611   Puerto
Alisa

Puerto del
Ponton   T   Espinama   21   Potes   Cabuérniga   574

Á   N621   B   C   A   Ramal
la Vic

Riaño   N621   1609   R   Embalse de
la Cohilla   47   39   9   Espinosa de
los Monteros   920
Los Torr

Embalse
de Riaño   Puerto de
San Glorio   1329   I   1718
VALNERA

1260   Bárcena de   1011
Puerto de
Escudo

C626   Puerto de
Piedrasluengas   Puerto de
Polombera   Pie de Concha   N   1000   Soncillo

1433   Besande   Reinosa   C6318   Corconte   Puerto de
Carrales   38   Villarcayo

Puerto
Monteviejo   987
Puerto Pozazal

Embalse de
Camporredondo   Cervera de
Pisuerga   1035   HIJEDO

Guardo   Cantorol   Pantano del Ebro   Escalada   94   1000
Puerto de la
Mazorra

13   Embalse
de Aguilar
de Campóo   14   Valdenoceda   N232

Saldaña   Herrera de
Pisuerga   1377
AMAYA   Tubilla
de Agua   Oña

Terradillos de
los Templarios   Portillo
del Fresno
1050

Ledigos   Montorio   Cernégula

Calzadilla
de la Cu   N120   Osorno   Villadiego

Carrión de   Villalcázar   E   F

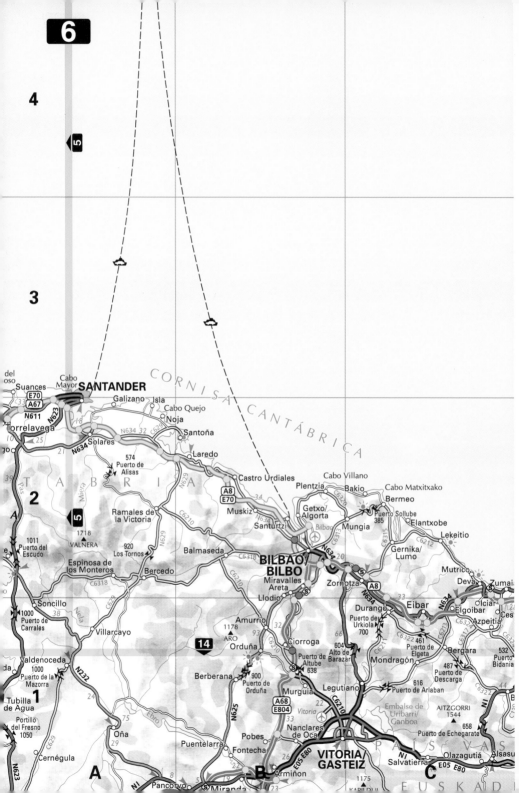

4

5

3

CORNISA CANTÁBRICA

del oso
Suances
E70
A67
N611
SANTANDER
Galizano
Isla
Cabo Quejo
Noja
Torrelavega
N634 32
Santoña
N634 Solares
Laredo
574 Puerto de Alisas
Castro Urdiales
Cabo Villano
Plentzia
Bakio
Cabo Matxitxako
Bermeo
2
Ramales de la Victoria
Muskiz
Getxo/ Algorta
Puerto Sollube
385
Elantxobe
5
1718
VALNERA
Santurtzi
Bilbao
Mungia
Lekeitio
1011 Puerto del Escudo
920
Los Tornos
Balmaseda
BILBAO/ BILBO
Gernika/ Lumo
Espinosa de los Monteros
Bercedo
Miravalles
Areta
Mutriko
Soncillo
Llodio
Zornotza
A8
Deva
Zumai
Eibar
N634
Olciar
1000 Puerto de Carrales
Villarcayo
Amurrio
Durango
Puerto de Urkiola 700
Elgoibar
Ces
14
ARO
Orduña
Ciorroga
604 Alto de Barazar
Puerto de Elgeta
461
Bergara
532 Puerto Bidania
Valdenoceda
Berberana
900 Puerto de Orduña
Puerto de Altube 638
Mondragón
487 Puerto de Descarga
1000 Puerto de la Mazorra
Murguía
Legutiano
616 Puerto de Arlaban
1
Tubilla de Agua
A68
E804
Vitoria
Puerto de Echegarate
AITZGORRI 1544
658
Portillo del Fresno 1050
Oña
Nanclares de Oca
Cernégula
Puentelarra
Fontecha
Pobes
Armiñon
VITORIA GASTEIZ
Salvatierra
Olazagutía
Alsasu
PAÍS VAS
EUSKAD

A
B
C

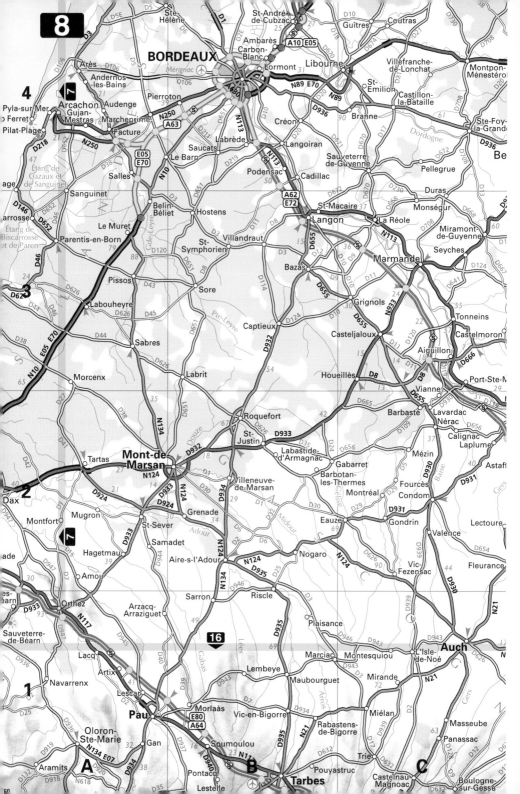

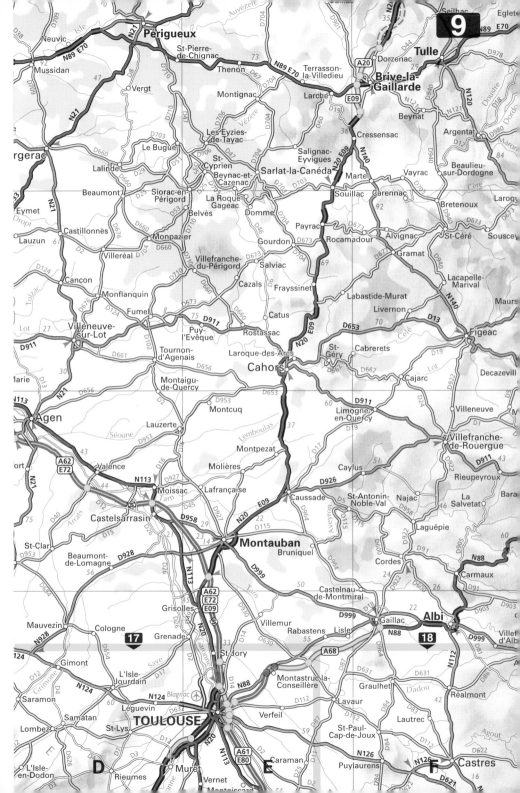

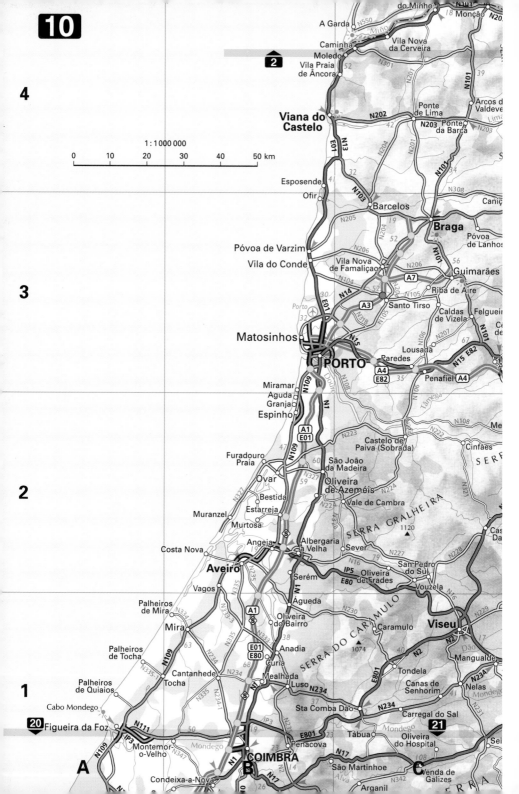

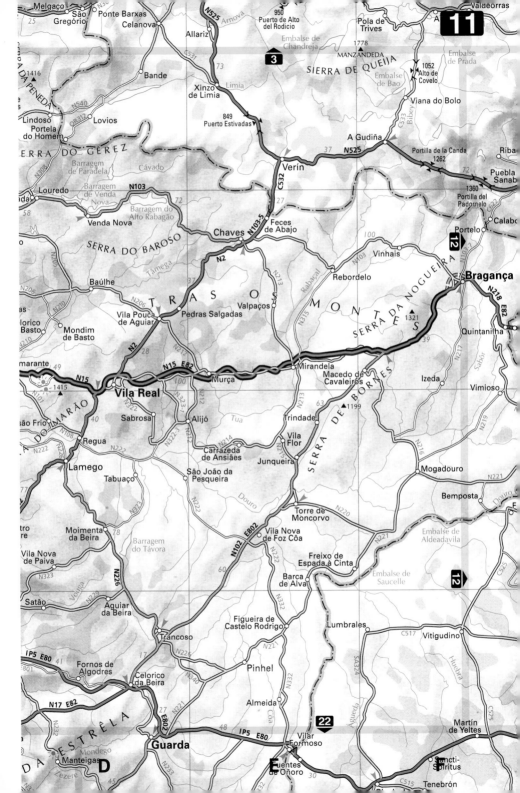

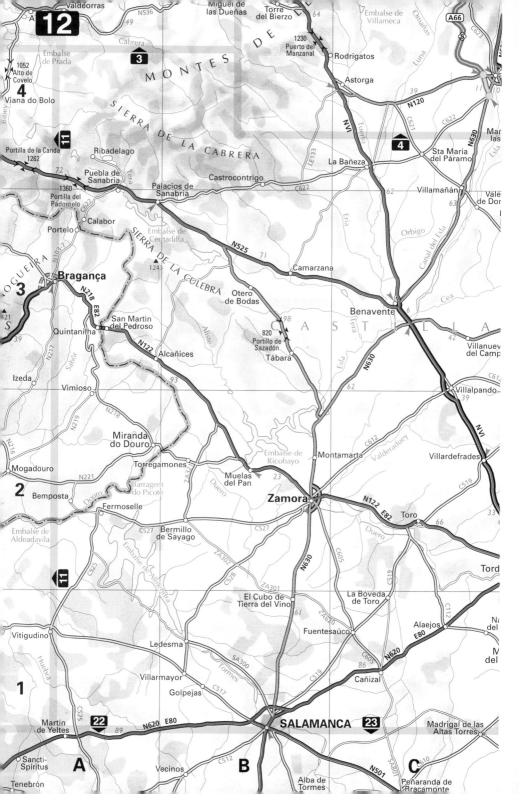

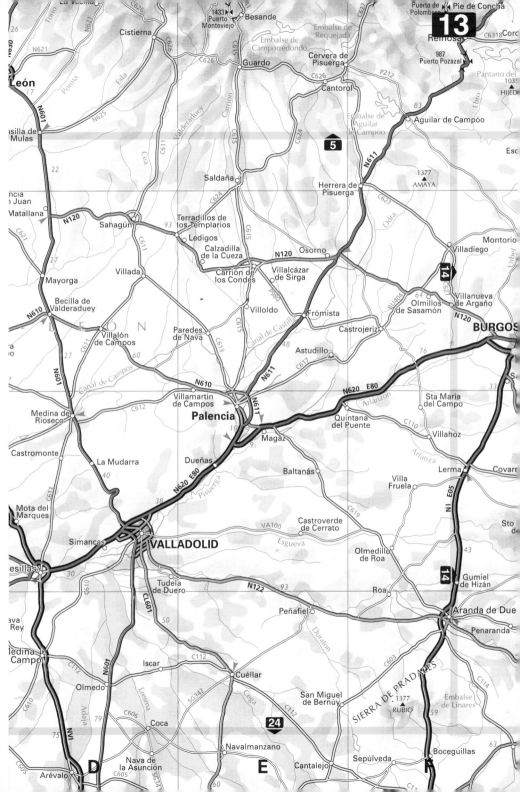

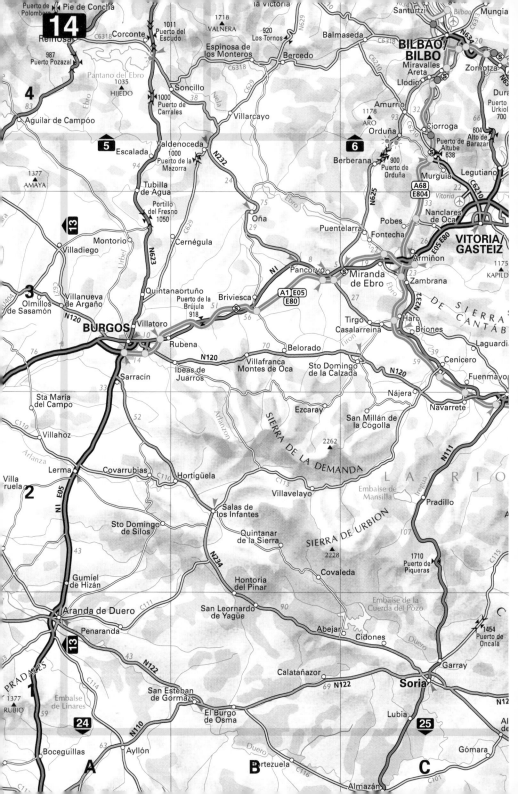

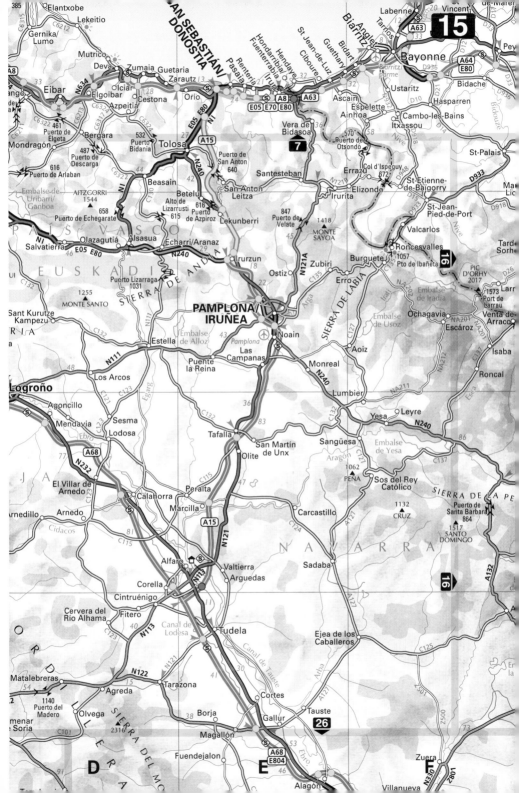

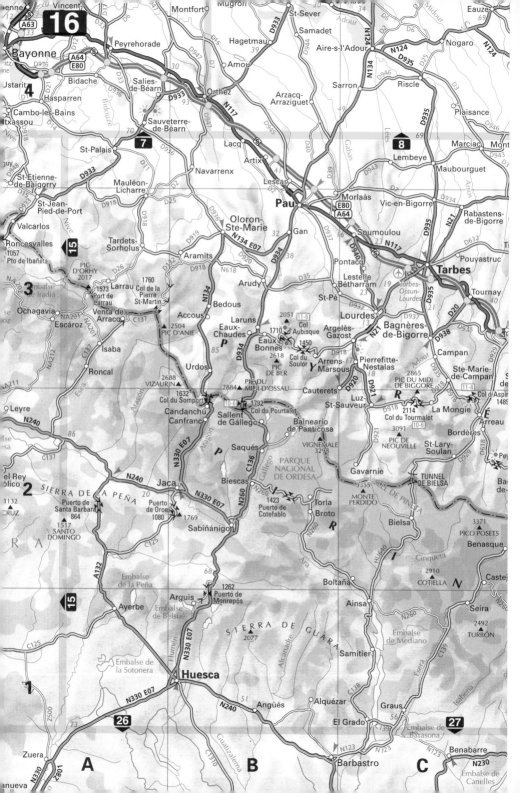

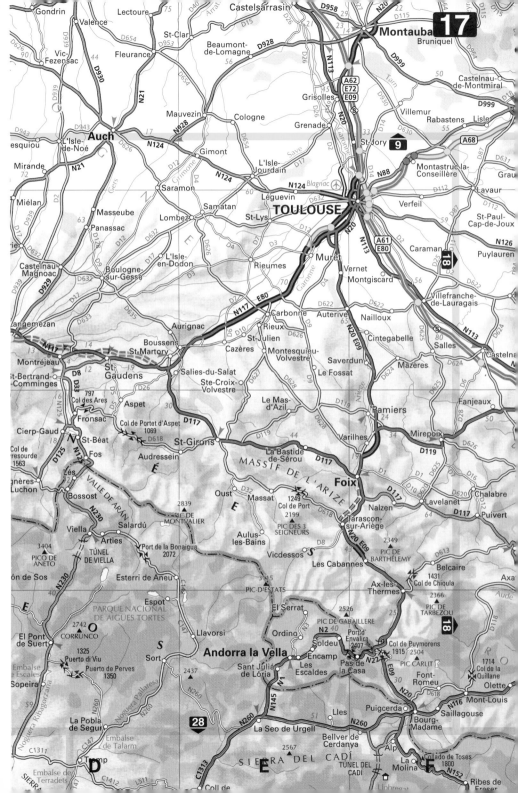

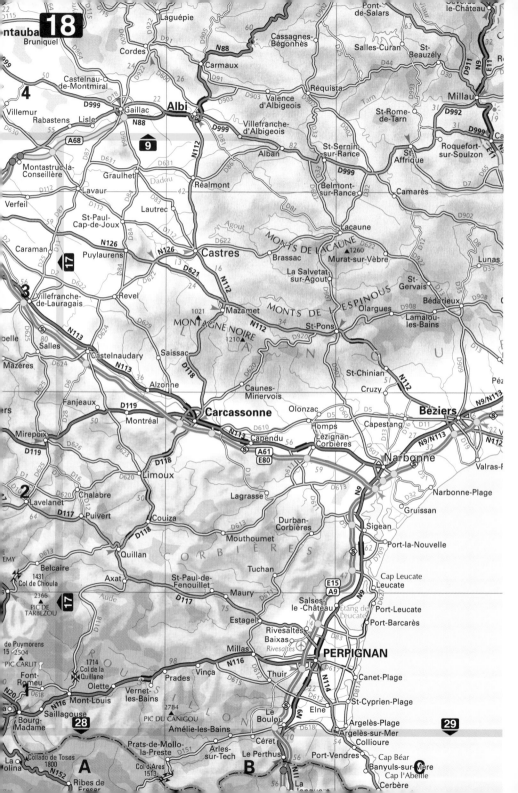

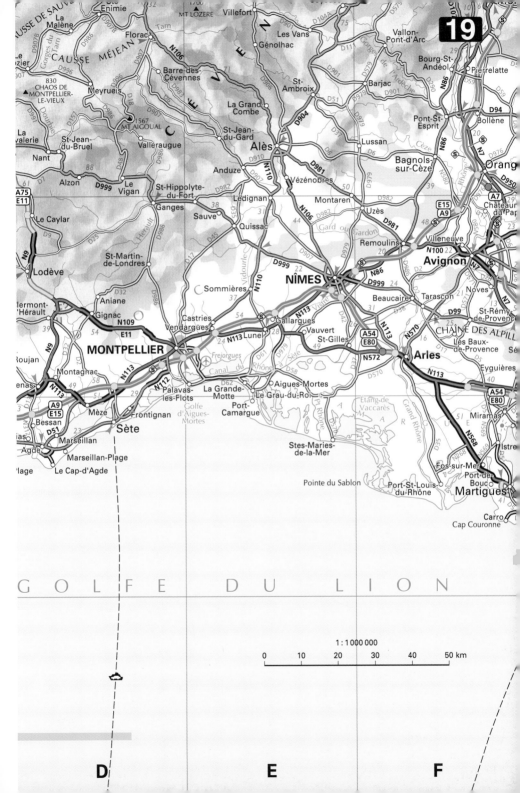

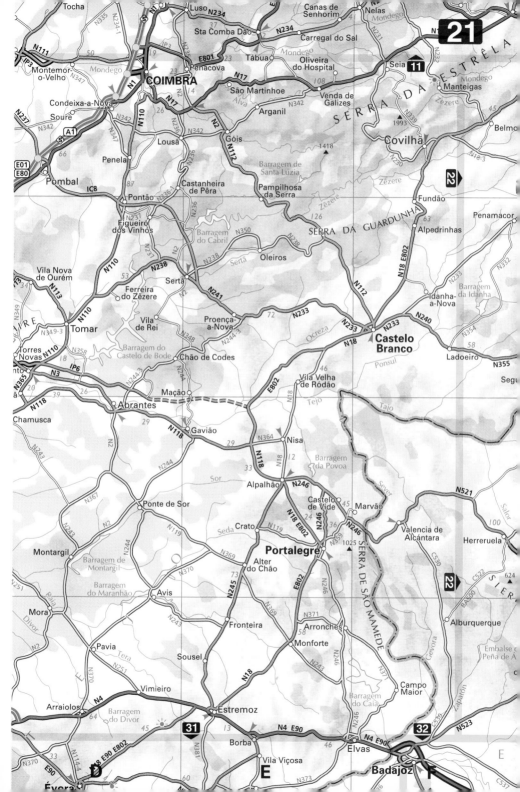

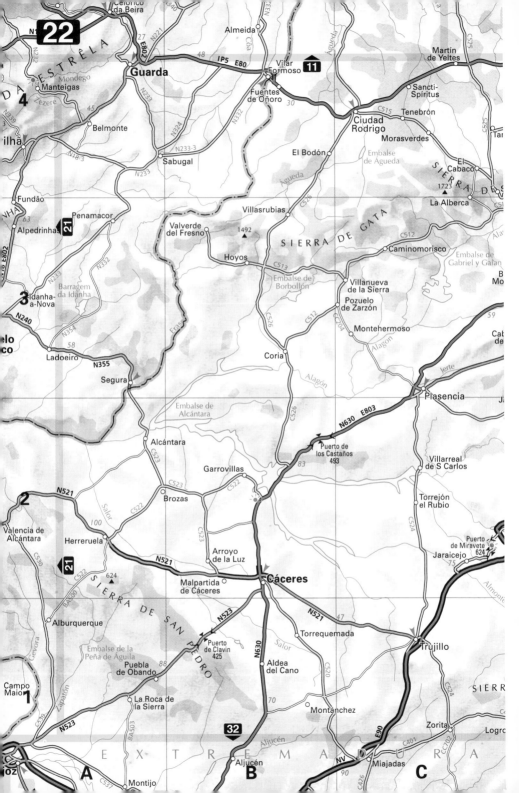

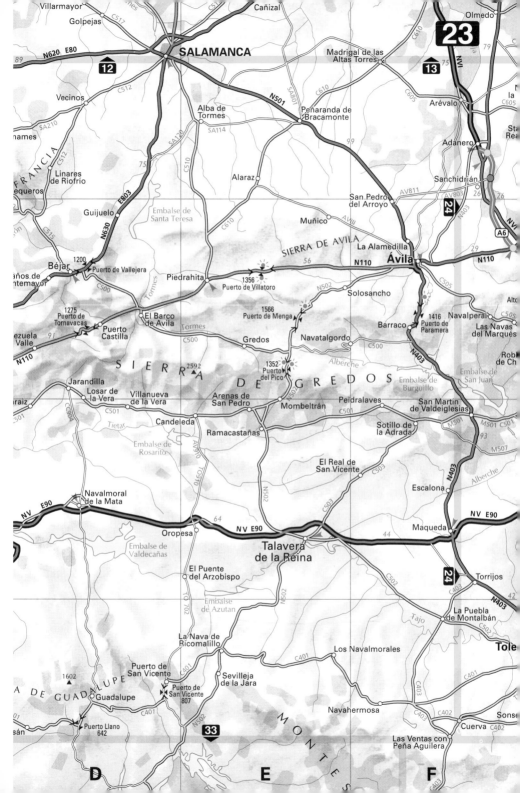

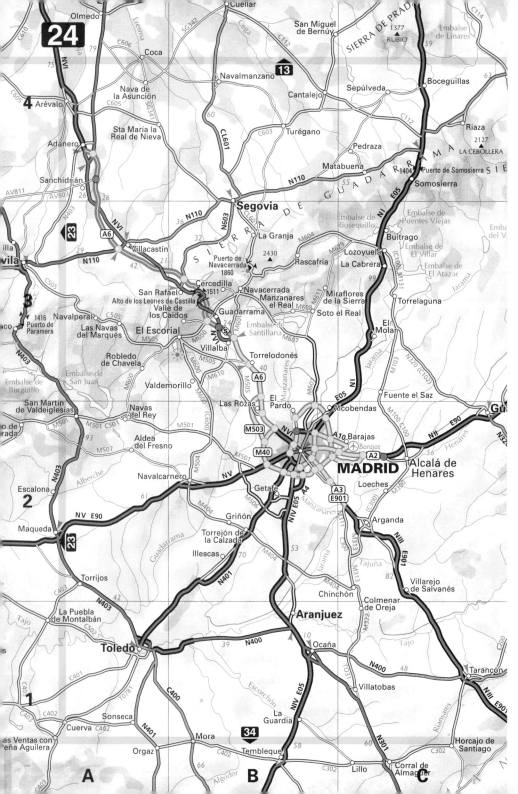

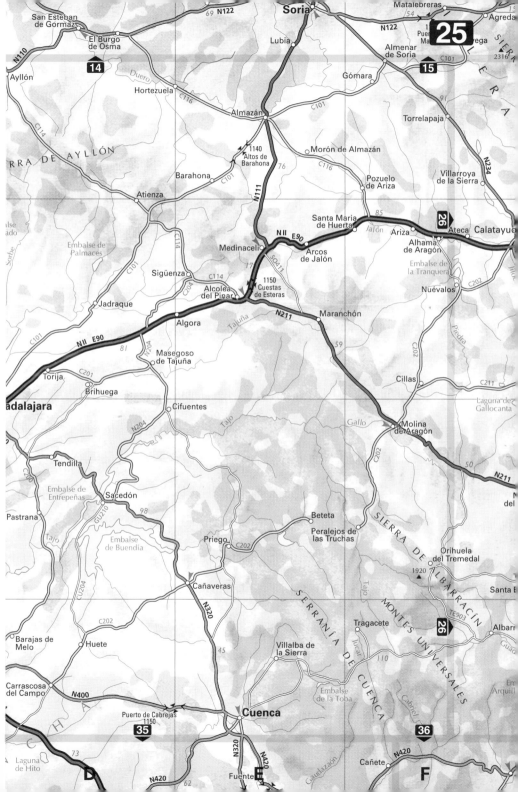

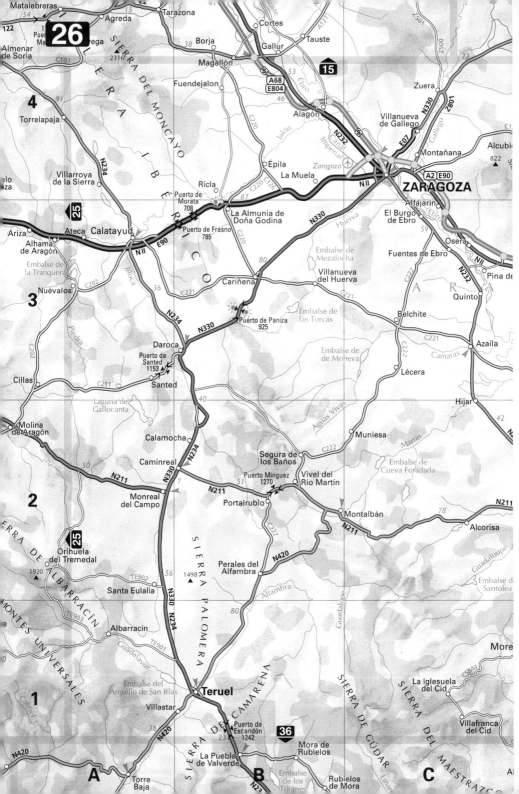

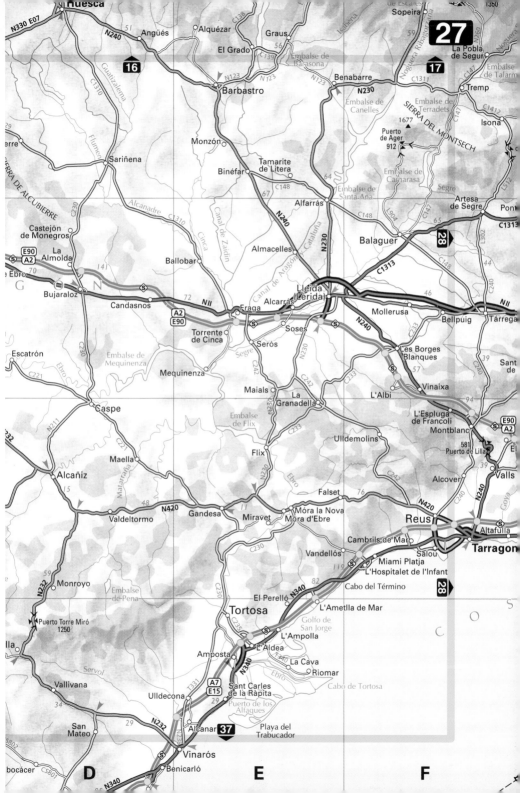

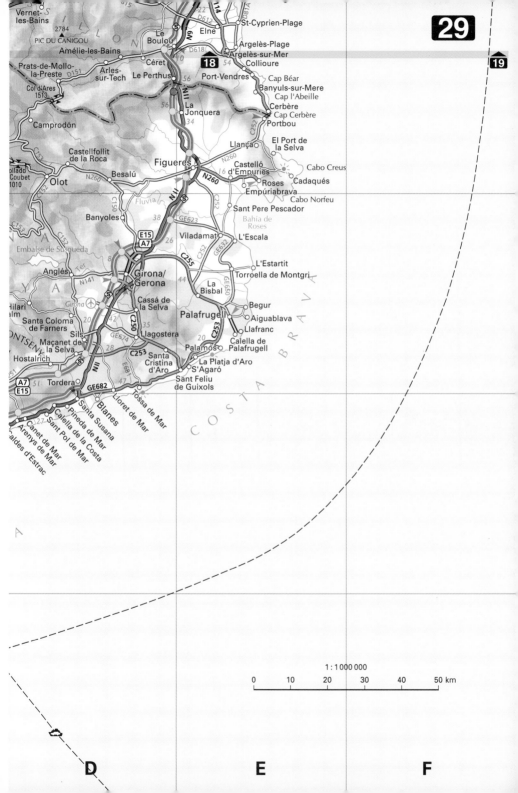

Vernet-
les-Bains
2784
PIC DU CANIGOU
Le Boulou
St-Cyprien-Plage
Elne
Amélie-les-Bains
Argelès-Plage
Céret
Argelès-sur-Mer
Prats-de-Mollo-
la-Preste
Arles-
sur-Tech
Le Perthus
54
Collioure
Col d'Ares
1513
56
Port-Vendres
Cap Béar
Camprodón
La
Jonquera
34
Banyuls-sur-Mere
Cap l'Abeille
Cerbère
Cap Cerbère
Portbou
Castellfollit
de la Roca
Figueres
Llançà
El Port de
la Selva
Olladö
Coubet
1010
Olot
N260
Besalú
N260
Castelló
d'Empúries
Cabo Creus
Banyoles
Fluvia
Roses
Empúriabrava
Cadaqués
Cabo Norfeu
Embalse de Susqueda
Viladamat
Sant Pere Pescador
Bahia de
Roses
L'Escala
Anglès
Girona/
Gerona
L'Estartit
Torroella de Montgri
Hilari
lm
Santa Coloma
de Farners
Cassà de
la Selva
La
Bisbal
Begur
Aiguablava
Palafrugell
Llafranc
Calella de
Palafrugell
Maçanet de
la Selva
Sils
Llagostera
Calella de
Palafrugell
Hostalrich
Santa
Cristina
d'Aro
Palamós
La Platja d'Aro
S'Agaró
Sant Feliu
de Guixols
Tordera
Lloret de Mar
Tossa de Mar
Santa Susana
Blanes
Pineda de Mar
Calella de la Costa
Sant Pol de Mar
Canet de Mar
Arenys de Mar
aldes d'Estrac

COSTA BRAVA

1 : 1 000 000
0   10   20   30   40   50 km

D   E   F

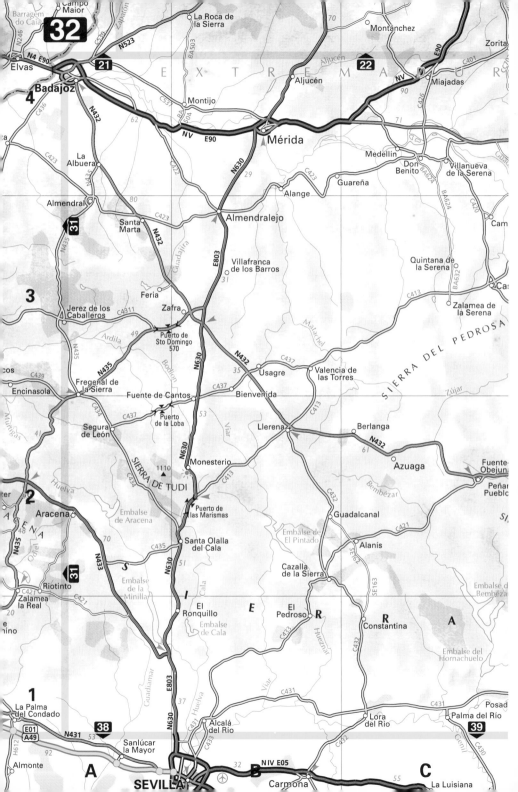

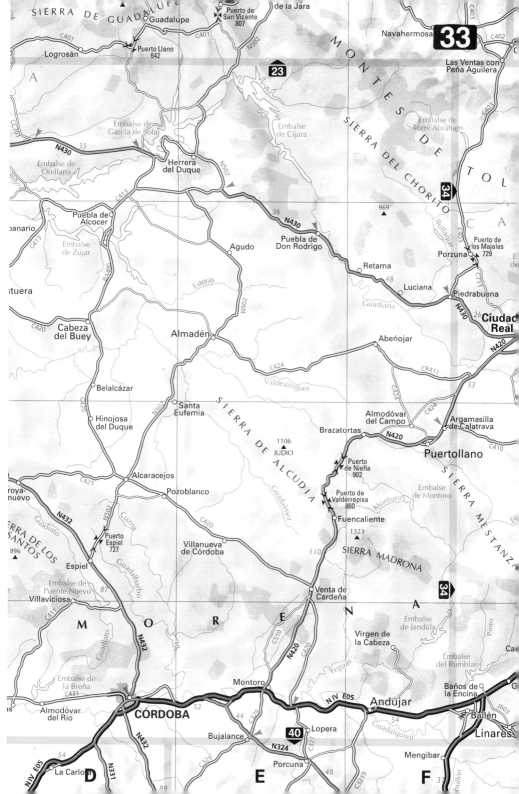

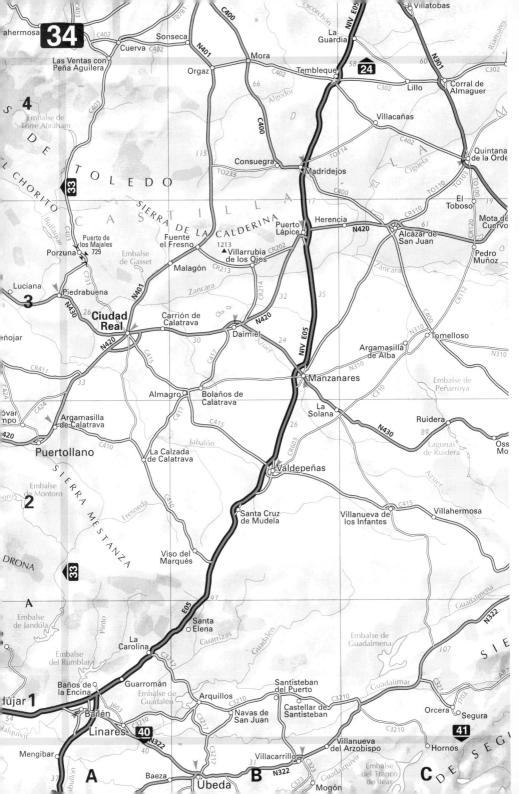

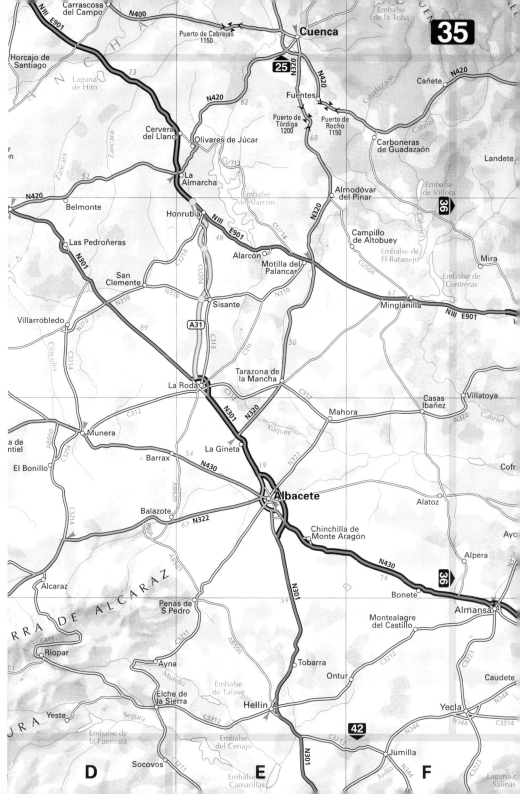

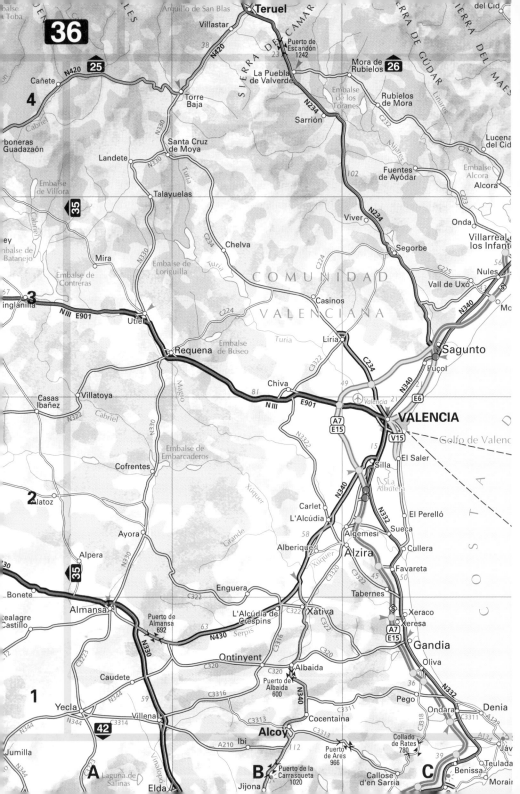

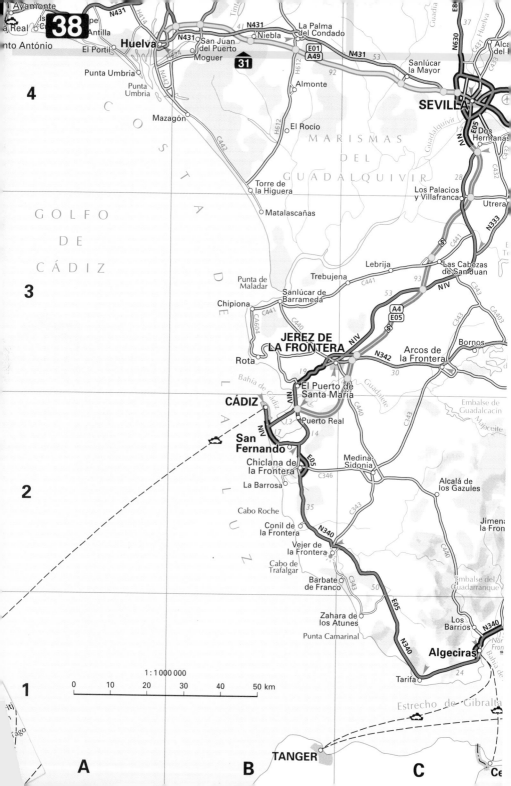

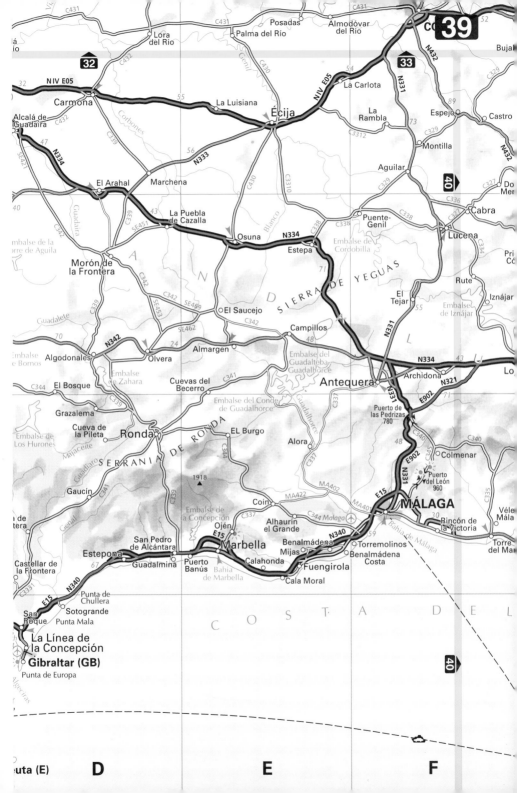

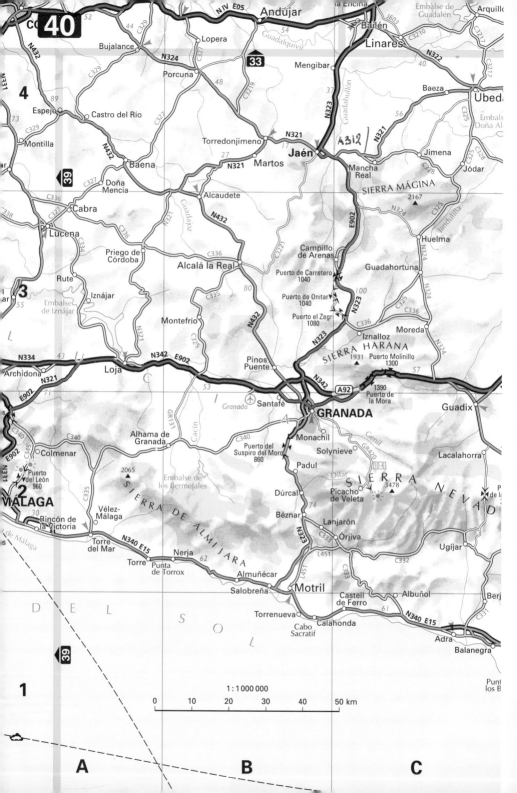

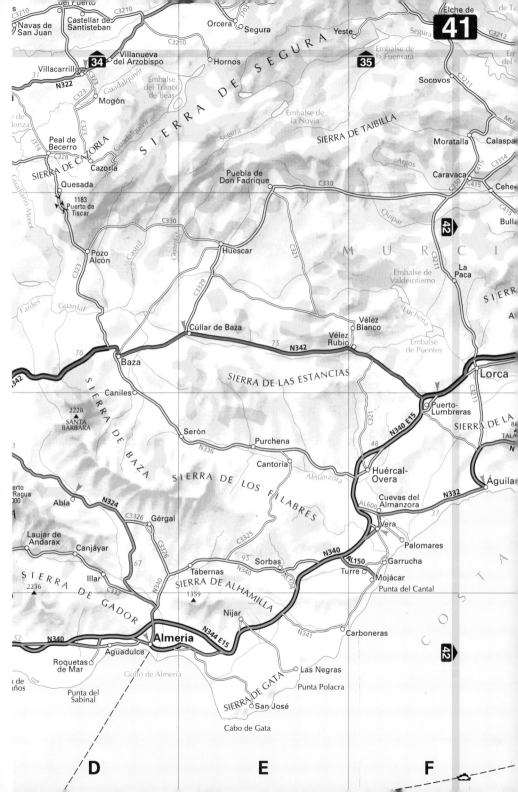

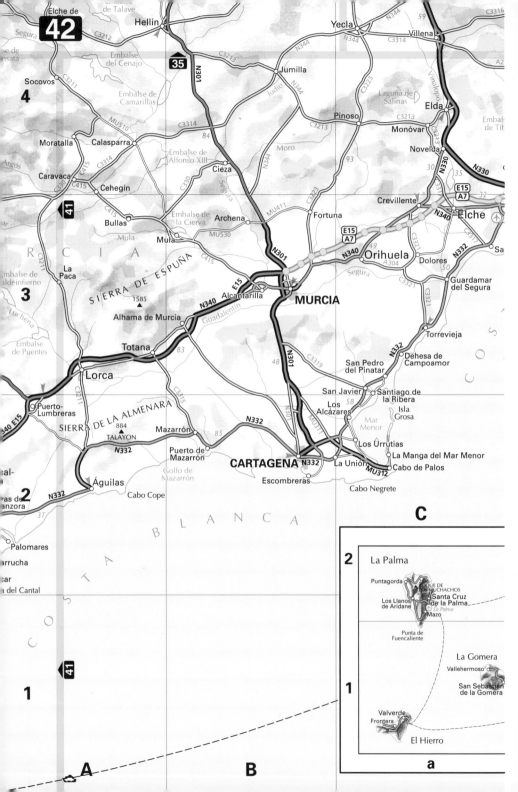

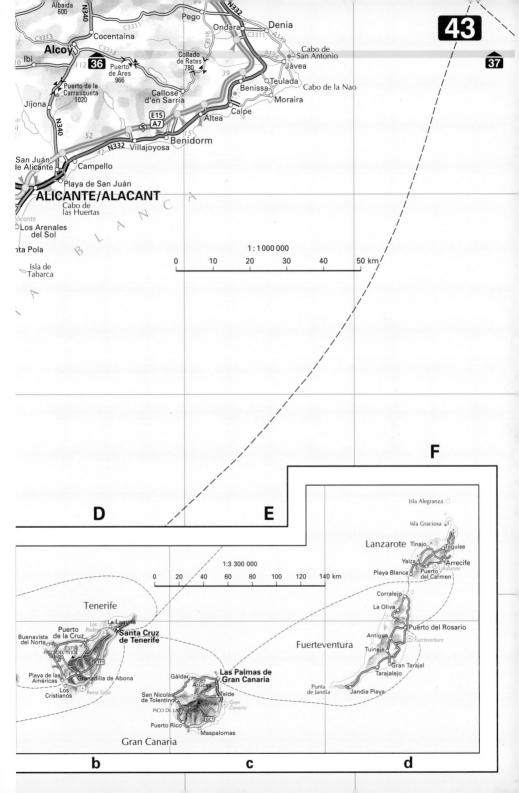

Albaida
600

N332

N340

C3311

Pego

Ondara

Denia

Cocentaina

C3313

Alcoy

Ibi

112

36

C3313

Puerto
de Ares
966

Callose
d'en Sarria

Collado
de Rates
780

C3311

Cabo de
San Antonio

Jávea

A134

39

Teulada

Cabo de la Nao

Benissa

Moraira

Puerto de la
Carrasqueta
1020

Jijona

N340

52

Villajoyosa

N332

42

E15
A7

Altea

Calpe

Benidorm

San Juán
de Alicante

Campello

Playa de San Juán

ALICANTE/ALACANT

Cabo de
las Huertas

Alicante

Los Arenales
del Sol

B L A N C A

nta Pola

Isla de
Tabarca

1 : 1 000 000

0   10   20   30   40   50 km

D

E

F

Isla Alegranza

Isla Graciosa

Lanzarote Tinajo

Teguise

1:3 300 000

0   20   40   60   80   100   120   140 km

Yaiza

Arrecife

Playa Blanca

Puerto
del Carmen

Lanzarote

Tenerife

Los
Rodeos

La Laguna

Corralejo

La Oliva

Buenavista
del Norte

Puerto
de la Cruz

**Santa Cruz
de Tenerife**

Puerto del Rosario

Fuerteventura

Antigua

Fuerteventura

PICO DEL TEIDE
3718

TF1

Tuineje

Playa de las
Américas

Granadilla de Abona

Los
Cristianos

Reina Sofía

Gáldar

**Las Palmas de
Gran Canaria**

Arucas

Telde

Gran Tarajal

Tarajalejo

Punta
de Jandía

Jandía Playa

San Nicolás
de Tolentino

PICO DE LAS NIEVES

Gran
Canaria

Puerto Rico

GC1

Maspalomas

Gran Canaria

b

c

d

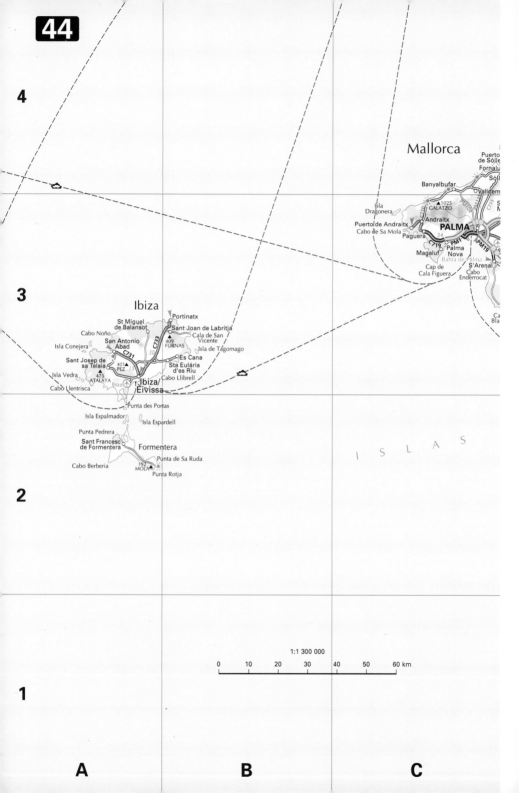

Menorca

Cabo Menorca
o de Bajoli
Cabo de
Cavallería

Ciutadella
Fornells

Cala Santandria
C721 24

Tamarinda
Santa
Galdana
Cabo de
Favaritx

Cabo d'Artrutx
Mercadal
350
TORO
Cabo de
Favaritx

Cala de
Santa Galdana
C721
21

Mahón

Calán
Porter
Mahón-
Menorca
Punta del Esperó

Villacarlos
S'Algar

Isla del Aire

BALEARES

Punta
Beca
Puerto de
Pollença
Cabo Formentor

Formentor

a Calobra
Pollença
Cabo del Pinar

PUIG
MAYOR
1448 1348
1068
MASANELLA
ALFABIA
Alcúdia

C710
9

Puerto de
Alcúdia

C713
12

Inca
28

Bahía de Pollença

Bahía de Alcúdia

Ca'n Picafort

PM27

Palma de
Mallorca

C715
48

Petrá

Artá
Cabo Freu

11

Cala
Ratjada

21
PM400

Cabo Pinar

Cala
Millor

Manacor

PM511

PM402

Punta de Amer

Llucmayor

Felanitx
PM512

Porto
Cristo

52

Campos
C717

C714

Colonia
Santa Jordi
Santanyi

Cabo de Salines

Isla Conejera

Isla Cabrera

E   F

Madeira

1 : 1 000 000

0   10   20   30   40   50 km

2

Ponta do
Tristão
Porto Moniz

Ponta de São Jorge
Santana

Ponta do
Pargo

São
Vicente

53

Faial

1862
PICO
RUIVO

Calheta

Machico
101

Ponta do Sol

Funchal

Ponta de
São
Lourenço

Ribeira Brava

Santa
Cruz

Câmara
de Lobos
Funchal

1

a   b

D

A

A Cañiza E 2 C1
A Coruña/La Coruña E 2 C4
A Estrada E 2 C2
A Garda E 2 A1
A Gudiña E 11 F4
A Rúa E 3 E1
Abejar E 14 C1
Abela P 30 C3
Abeñojar E 33 F3
Abla E 41 D2
Abrantes P 21 D2
Accous F 16 B3
Adanero E 24 A4
Adra E 40 C1
Agde F 19 D2
Agen F 9 D2
Agoncillo E 15 D2
Agreda E 15 D1
Aguadulce E 41 D1
Aguda P 10 B2
Agudo E 33 E3
Águeda P 10 B1
Aguiar da Beira P 11 D1
Aguilar E 39 F4
Aguilar de Campóo E 5 E1
Águilas E 42 A2
Aiguablava E 29 E3
Aigues-Mortes F 19 E3
Aiguillon F 8 C3
Ainhoa F 7 E1
Ainsa E 16 C1
Aire-sur-l'Adour F 8 B2
Alacant (Alicante) E 43 D4
Alaejos E 12 C1
Alagón E 26 B4
Alandroal P 31 E4
Alange E 32 B4
Alanis E 32 C2
Alaraz E 23 E4
Alarcón E 35 E3
Alatoz E 35 F2
Alba de Tormes E 23 E4
Albacete E 35 E2
Albaida E 36 B1
Alban F 18 B4
Albarracín E 26 A1
Albergaria a Velha P 10 B2
Alberique E 36 B2
Albi F 9 F1
Albocácer E 37 D4
Albufeira P 30 B1
Albuñol E 40 C1
Alburquerque E 21 F1
Alcácer do Sal P 30 C4
Alcáçovas P 31 D4
Alcalá de Chivert E 37 D4
Alcalá de Guadaira E 39 D4
Alcalá de Henares E 24 C2
Alcalá de los Gazules E 38 C2
Alcalá del Río E 32 B1
Alcalá la Real E 40 B3
Alcanar E 27 E1
Alcanede P 20 C3
Alcanena P 20 C3
Alcañices E 12 A3
Alcañiz E 27 D2
Alcántara E 22 A2
Alcantarilla E 42 B3
Alcaracejos E 33 D2
Alcaraz E 35 D2
Alcarràs E 27 E3
Alcaudete E 40 B3

Alcázar de San Juan E 34 C3
Alcobaça P 20 C3
Alcobendas E 24 B2
Alcoceber E 37 D4
Alcochete P 20 B1
Alcolea del Pinar E 25 E3
Alcora E 36 C4
Alcorisa E 26 C2
Alcoutim P 31 D2
Alcover E 28 A2
Alcoy E 36 B1
Alcubierre E 27 D4
Alcúdia E 45 D4
Aldea del Cano E 22 B1
Aldea del Fresno E 24 A2
Alés F 19 E4
Alfajarín E 26 C3
Alfambras P 30 B2
Alfaro E 15 E2
Alfarràs E 27 E3
Alfeizerão P 20 C3
Algeciras E 38 C1
Algemesí E 36 C2
Algodonales E 39 D3
Algora E 25 E3
Algorta/Getxo E 6 B2
Alhama de Aragón E 25 F3
Alhama de Granada E 40 B2
Alhama de Murcia E 42 B3
Alhaurín el Grande E 39 E2
Alicante (Alacant) E 43 D4
Alijó P 11 E2
Aljezur P 30 B2
Aljubarrota P 20 C3
Aljucén E 32 B4
Aljustrel P 30 C3
Allariz E 2 C1
Almacelles E 27 E3
Almadén E 33 E3
Almagro E 34 B3
Almansa E 36 A1
Almargen E 39 E3
Almazán E 25 E4
Almazora E 37 D3
Almeida P 11 E1
Almeirim P 20 C2
Almenar de Soria E 25 F4
Almendral E 32 A3
Almendralejo E 32 B3
Almería E 41 D1
Almodóvar P 30 C2
Almodóvar del Campo E 33 F2
Almodóvar del Pinar E 35 E4
Almodóvar del Río E 33 D1
Almograve P 30 B3
Almonaster la Real E 31 F2
Almonte E 38 B4
Almuñécar E 40 B2
Alora E 39 E2
Alosno E 31 E2
Alp E 28 C4
Alpalhão P 21 E2
Alpedrinhas P 21 F3
Alpera E 36 A2
Alquézar E 16 B1
Alsasua E 15 D3
Altafulla E 28 A2
Altea E 43 E4
Alter do Chão P 21 E2
Alvalade P 30 C3
Alvignac F 9 F3
Alvito P 31 D3
Alvor P 30 B1
Alzira E 36 C2
Alzon F 19 D4
Alzonne F 18 A3

Amarante P 10 C3
Amareleja P 31 E3
Ambarès F 8 B4
Ambasmestas E 3 E1
Ameixial P 30 C2
Amélie-les-Bains F 29 D4
Amou F 8 A2
Amposta E 27 E1
Amurria E 6 B1
Anadia P 10 B1
Andernos-les-Bains F 8 A4
Andorra la Vella AND 17 E1
Andraitx E 44 C3
Andújar E 33 F1
Anduze F 19 E4
Angeja P 10 B2
Anglés E 29 D3
Anglet F 7 E2
Angüés E 16 B1
Aniane F 19 D3
Antequera E 39 F3
Antigua E 43 d1
Aoiz E 15 F3
Aracena E 32 A2
Aramits F 16 B3
Aranaz/Echarri E 15 D3
Aranda de Duero E 13 F1
Aranjuez E 24 B1
Arcachon F 7 F4
Archena E 42 B3
Archidona E 39 F3
Arcos de Jalón E 25 E3
Arcos de la Frontera E 38 C3
Arcos de Valdeves P 10 C4
Arenas E 5 D3
Arenas de San Pedro E 23 E2
Arenys de Mar E 29 D2
Ares E 3 D4
Arès F 8 A4
Areta E 6 B2
Arévalo E 24 A4
Argamasilla de Alba E 34 C3
Argamasilla de Calatrava E 33 F2
Arganda E 24 C2
Arganil P 21 E4
Argelès-Gazost F 16 C3
Argelès-Plage F 18 C1
Argelès-sur-Mer F 18 C1
Argentat F 9 F4
Arguedas E 15 E2
Arguis E 16 B1
Ariza E 25 F3
Arles F 19 F3
Arles-sur-Tech F 29 D4
Armação de Pera P 30 B1
Armiñon E 14 C3
Arnedillo E 15 D2
Arnedo E 15 D2
Arquillos E 34 B1
Arrabal (Oia) E 2 A1
Arraiolos P 21 D1
Arreau F 16 C2
Arrecife E 43 d2
Arrens-Marsous F 16 B3
Arrifana P 30 A2
Arriondas E 5 D3
Arronches P 21 E1
Arroyo de la Luz E 22 B2
Arruda dos Vinhos P 20 B2
Artá E 45 D3
Artesa de Segre E 28 A3
Arties E 17 D2
Artix F 16 B4
Arucas E 43 c1
Arudy F 16 B3
Arzacq-Arraziguet F 8 A1

Arzúa *E*	**2**	C3
Ascain *F*	**7**	E1
Aspet *F*	**17**	D2
Astaffort *F*	**9**	D2
Astorga *E*	**4**	B1
Astudillo *E*	**13**	E3
Ateca *E*	**26**	A3
Atienza *E*	**25**	D3
Auch *F*	**8**	C1
Audenge *F*	**8**	A4
Audressein *F*	**17**	E2
Aulus-les-Bains *F*	**17**	E2
Aurignac *F*	**17**	D3
Auterive *F*	**17**	E3
Aveiras de Cima *P*	**20**	C2
Aveiro *P*	**10**	B2
Avignon *F*	**19**	F3
Ávila *E*	**23**	F3
Avilés *E*	**4**	C4
Avis *P*	**21**	D1
Ax-les-Thermes *F*	**17**	F2
Axat *F*	**18**	A2
Ayamonte *E*	**31**	D1
Ayerbe *E*	**16**	A1
Ayllón *E*	**25**	D4
Ayna *E*	**35**	D1
Ayora *E*	**36**	A2

Azaila *E*	**26**	C3
Azambuja *P*	**20**	C2
Azinheira dos Barros *P*	**30**	C3
Azpeitia *E*	**6**	C1
Azuaga *E*	**32**	C2

B

Baamonde *E*	**3**	D3
Badajoz *E*	**32**	A4
Badalona *E*	**28**	C2
Baena *E*	**40**	A4
Baeza *E*	**40**	C4
Bagá *E*	**28**	C4
Bagnères-de-Bigorre *F*	**16**	C3
Bagnères-de-Luchon *F*	**17**	D2
Bagnols-sur-Cèze *F*	**19**	F4
Bailén *E*	**34**	A1
Baio *E*	**2**	B3
Baiona *E*	**2**	A1
Baixas *F*	**18**	B1
Bakio *E*	**6**	C2
Balaguer *E*	**27**	F3
Balanegra *E*	**40**	C1
Balazote *E*	**35**	D2

Baleira/O Cádabo *E*	**3**	E2
Ballobar *E*	**27**	E3
Balmaseda *E*	**6**	B2
Balneario de Panticosa *E*	**16**	B2
Balsareny *E*	**28**	B3
Baltanás *E*	**13**	E2
Bande *E*	**11**	D4
Baños de la Encina *E*	**34**	A1
Baños de Montemayor *E*	**23**	D3
Banyalbufar *E*	**44**	C4
Banyoles *E*	**29**	D3
Banyuls-sur-Mer *F*	**29**	E4
Barahona *E*	**25**	E4
Barajas *E*	**24**	C2
Barajas de Melo *E*	**25**	D1
Barbaste *F*	**8**	C2
Barbastro *E*	**27**	E4
Barbate de Franco *E*	**38**	C2
Barbotan-les-Thermes *F*	**8**	B2
Barca de Alva *P*	**11**	E2
Barcelona *E*	**28**	C2
Barcelos *P*	**10**	C3
Bárcena de Pie de Concha *E*	**5**	F2
Barjac *F*	**19**	F4
Barraco *E*	**23**	F3
Barranco do Velho *P*	**30**	C1
Barrancos *P*	**31**	F3

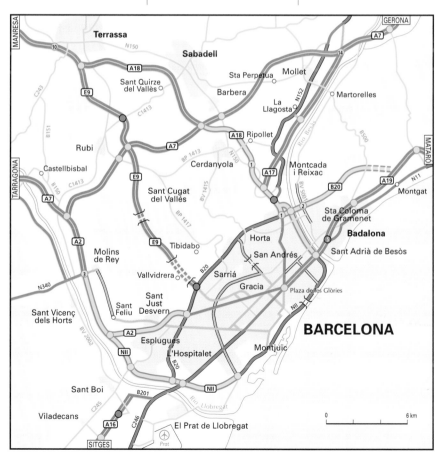

Barrax E	35	D2
Barre-des-Cévennes F	19	D4
Barreiro P	20	B1
Barreiros/San Cosme E	3	E3
Bassella E	28	B4
Batalha P	20	C3
Baúlhe P	11	D3
Bayonne F	7	E2
Baza E	41	D3
Bazas F	8	B3
Beasain E	15	D4
Beaucaire F	19	F3
Beaulieu-sur-Dordogne F	9	F4
Beaumont F	9	D3
Beaumont-de-Lomagne F	9	D2
Becerreá E	3	E2
Becilla de Valderaduey E	13	D3
Bédarieux F	18	C3
Bedous F	16	B3
Begur E	29	E3
Beja P	31	D3
Béjar E	23	D3
Belalcázar E	33	D3
Belcaire F	17	F2
Belchite E	26	C3
Belin-Béliet F	8	A3
Bellpuig E	27	F3
Bellver de Cerdanya E	28	C4
Belmont-sur-Rance F	18	C3
Belmonte E	4	B3
Belmonte E	35	D3
Belmonte E	22	A4
Belorado E	14	B3
Belvès F	9	E3
Bembibre E	4	A2
Bemposta P	12	A2
Benabarre E	27	E4
Benalmádena E	39	E2
Benalmádena Costa E	39	E2
Benasque E	16	C2
Benavente E	12	C3
Benavente P	20	C2
Benicarló E	37	E4
Benicasim E	37	D3
Benidorm E	43	D4
Benissa E	43	E4
Bensafrim P	30	B2
Berberana E	14	C4
Bercedo E	6	A2
Berga E	28	C4
Bergara E	6	C1
Bergerac F	9	D4
Berja E	40	C1
Berlanga E	32	C2
Bermeo E	6	C2
Bermillo de Sayago E	12	B2
Besalú E	29	D4
Besande E	5	D2
Bessan F	19	D2
Bestida P	10	B2
Betanzos E	2	C3
Betelu E	15	E3
Beteta E	25	E2
Beynac-et-Cazenac F	9	E4
Beynat F	9	E4
Béziers F	18	C2
Béznar E	40	B2
Biarritz F	7	E2
Bias F	7	F3
Bidache F	7	E2
Bidart F	7	E2
Bielsa E	16	C2
Bienvenida E	32	B3
Biescas E	16	B2
Bilbao/Bilbo E	6	B2
Bilbo/Bilbao E	6	B2
Binéfar E	27	E4
Biscarrosse F	7	F3
Biscarrosse-Plage F	7	F4
Blanes E	29	D2
Boal E	4	A4
Boceguillas E	24	C4
Bolaños de Calatrava E	34	B3
Bollène F	19	F4
Boltaña E	16	C2
Bombarral P	20	B3
Boñar E	4	C2
Bonete E	35	F2
Borba P	31	E4
Bordeaux F	8	B4
Bordeira P	30	A2
Bordères F	16	C2
Borja E	15	E1
Bornos E	38	C3
Bossost E	17	D2
Boulogne-sur-Gesse F	17	D3
Bourg F	8	B4
Bourg-Madame F	17	F1
Bourg-St-Andéol F	19	F4
Boussens F	17	E3
Braga P	10	C3
Bragança P	11	F3
Branne F	8	C4
Brassac F	18	B3
Brazatortas E	33	F2
Bretenoux F	9	F3
Brihuega E	25	D3
Briones E	14	C3
Brive-la-Gaillarde F	9	F4
Briviesca E	14	B3
Broto E	16	B2
Brozas E	22	A2
Bruniquel F	9	E2
Buenavista del Norte E	43	b1
Buitrago E	24	C3
Bujalance E	33	E1
Bujaraloz E	27	D3
Bullas E	42	A3
Burela E	3	E4
Burgau P	30	B1
Burgos E	14	A3
Burguete E	15	F3
Burriana E	37	D3

C

Ca'n Picafort E	45	D3
Cabañaquinta E	4	C3
Cabañas E	3	D4
Cabeza del Buey E	33	D3
Cabezas Rubias E	31	E2
Cabezón de la Sal E	5	E2
Cabezuela del Valle E	23	D3
Cabo de Palos E	42	C2
Cabo de San Vicente P	30	A1
Cabra E	40	A3
Cabreiros E	3	D3
Cabrerets F	9	F3
Cabuérniga E	5	E2
Cáceres E	22	B2
Cachopo P	30	C1
Cadaqués E	29	E4
Cadillac F	8	B4
Cádiz E	38	B2
Cahors F	9	E3
Cajarc F	9	F3
Cala Millor E	45	D3
Cala Moral E	39	E2
Cala Ratjada E	45	E3
Calabor E	12	A3
Calaf E	28	B3
Calafell E	28	B2
Calahonda E	39	E2
Calahonda E	40	B1
Calahorra E	15	D2
Calamocha E	26	B2
Calán Porter E	45	F3
Calasparra E	42	A4
Calatañazor E	14	B1
Calatayud E	26	A3
Caldas da Rainha P	20	B3
Caldas de Reis E	2	B2
Caldas de Vizela P	10	C3
Caldes d'Estrac E	29	D2
Caldes de Montbui E	28	C3
Calella de la Costa E	29	D2
Calella de Palafrugell E	29	E3
Calheta P	45	a1
Calignac F	8	C2
Callose d'En Sarria E	43	D4
Calpe E	43	E4
Calzadilla de la Cueza E	13	E3
Câmara de Lobos P	45	a1
Camarès F	18	C3
Camariñas E	2	B4
Camarzana E	12	B3
Cambados E	2	B2
Cambeo E	2	C1
Cambo-les-Bains F	7	E1
Cambre E	2	C3
Cambrils de Mar E	27	F2
Caminha P	2	A1
Caminomorisco E	22	C3
Caminreal E	26	B2
Campan F	16	C3
Campanario E	32	C3
Campello E	43	D4
Campillo de Altobuey E	35	F3
Campillo de Arenas E	40	C3
Campillos E	39	E3
Campo de Caso E	4	C3
Campo Maior P	21	F1
Campodón E	29	D4
Campomanes E	4	C3
Campos E	45	D3
Canas de Senhorim P	10	C1
Cañaveras E	25	E2
Cancon F	9	D3
Candanchú E	16	B2
Candás E	4	C4
Candasnos E	27	D3
Candeleda E	23	E2
Canero E	4	B4
Canet de Mar E	29	D2
Canet-Plage F	18	C1
Cañete E	35	F4
Canfranc E	16	B2
Cangas E	2	B2
Cangas de Narcea E	4	A3
Cangas de Onis E	5	D3
Cañiçada P	11	D3
Caniles E	41	D3
Cañizal E	12	C1
Canjáyar E	41	D2
Cantalejo E	24	B4
Cantanhede P	10	B1
Cantoria E	41	E2
Cantorol E	5	E1
Cap Ferret F	7	F4
Capbreton F	7	E2
Capendu F	18	B2
Capestang F	18	C2
Captieux F	8	B3
Caraman F	17	F3
Caramulo P	10	C1
Caranga E	4	B3

Caravaca E 42 A4
Carballiño E 2 C2
Carballo E 2 C3
Carbon-Blanc F 8 B4
Carboneras E 41 E1
Carboneras de Guadazaón E 35 F4
Carbonne F 17 E3
Carcassonne F 18 B2
Càrcastillo E 15 E2
Carcavelos P 20 A2
Cardedeu E 28 C3
Cardona E 28 B3
Carennac F 9 F3
Cariñena E 26 B3
Carlet E 36 B2
Carmaux F 9 F2
Carmona E 39 D4
Carnota E 2 B3
Carrascosa del Campo E 25 D1
Carrazeda de Ansiães P 11 E2
Carregado P 20 B2
Carregal do Sal P 10 C1
Carrión de Calatrava E 34 A3
Carrión de los Condes E 13 E3
Carro F 19 F2
Cartagena E 42 B2
Cartaxó P 20 C2
Carvoeiro P 30 B1
Casalarreina E 14 C3
Casas Ibañez E 35 F2
Cascais P 20 A2
Casinos E 36 B3
Caspe E 27 D2
Cassá de la Selva E 29 D3
Cassagnes-Bégonhès F 18 B4
Castanheira de Pêra P 21 D4
Castejón de Monegros E 27 D3
Castejón de Sos E 16 C2
Castelejo E 30 A2
Casteljaloux F 8 C3
Castell de Ferro E 40 C1
Castellar de la Frontera E 39 D2
Castellar de Santisteban E 34 B1
Castelldefels E 28 B2
Castellfollit de la Roca E 29 D4
Castelló d'Empuries E 29 E4
Castellón de la Plana E 37 D3
Castelmoron E 8 C3
Castelnau-de-Montmiral F 9 F2
Castelnau-Magnoac F 17 D3
Castelnaudary F 18 A3
Castelo Branco P 21 F3
Castelo de Paiva (Sobrada) P .. 10 C2
Castelo de Vide P 21 E2
Castelsarrasin F 9 D2
Castets F 7 F2
Castillon-la-Bataille F 8 C4
Castillonnès F 9 D3
Castres F 18 B3
Castries F 19 E3
Castro Caldelas E 3 D1
Castro Daire P 10 C2
Castro del Río E 40 A4
Castro Marim P 31 D1
Castro Urdiales E 6 B2
Castro Verde P 30 C2
Castrocontrigo E 12 B4
Castrojeriz E 13 F3
Castromonte E 13 D2
Castropol E 3 F3
Castroverde de Cerrato E 13 E2
Castuera E 32 C3
Catus F 9 E3
Caudete E 36 A1
Caunes-Minervois F 18 B3
Caussade F 9 E2

Cauterets F 16 C3
Caylus F 9 F2
Cazalla de la Sierra E 32 B2
Cazals F 9 E3
Cazères F 17 E3
Cazorla E 41 D4
Cebreiro E 3 E2
Cedeira E 3 D4
Cehegín E 42 A4
Celanova E 2 C1
Celorico da Beira P 11 D1
Celorico de Basto P 11 D3
Cenicero E 14 C3
Cerbère F 29 E4
Cercal P 30 B3
Cercal P 20 B2
Cercedilla E 24 B3
Céret F 29 D4
Cernégula E 14 B3
Cervera E 28 A3
Cervera de Pisuerga E 5 E2
Cervera del Llano E 35 E4
Cervera del Río Alhama E 15 D1
Cervo E 3 E4
Cestona E 6 C1
Ceuta E 38 C1
Chalabre F 18 A2
Chamusca P 20 C2
Chantada E 3 D2
Chão de Codes P 21 D3
Châteauneuf-du-Pape F 19 F3
Chaves P 11 E3
Chelva E 36 B3
Chiclana de la Frontera E 38 B2
Chinchilla de Monte Aragón E .. 35 E2
Chinchón E 24 C2
Chipiona E 38 B3
Chiva E 36 B3
Ciboure F 7 D2
Cidones E 14 C1
Cierp-Gaud F 17 D2
Cieza E 42 B4
Cifuentes E 25 D2
Cillas E 25 F3
Cinfães P 10 C2
Cintegabelle F 17 F3
Cintruénigo E 15 D1
Ciorroga P 6 B1
Cistierna E 5 D2
Ciudad Real E 34 A3
Ciudad Rodrigo E 22 C4
Ciutadella E 45 E4
Clermont-l'Hérault F 19 D3
Coca E 13 D1
Cocentaina E 36 B1
Cofrentes E 36 A2
Coimbra P 21 D4
Coín E 39 E2
Coina P 20 B1
Colares P 20 A2
Coll de Nargó E 28 B4
Collioure F 29 E4
Colmenar E 39 F2
Colmenar de Oreja E 24 C1
Cologne F 9 D1
Colonia Santa Jordi E 45 D3
Colunga E 5 D3
Coma-ruga E 28 B2
Comillas E 5 E3
Comporta P 30 C4
Concurbión E 2 B3
Condeixa-a-Nova P 21 D4
Condom F 8 C2
Conil de la Frontera E 38 B2
Constantina E 32 C1
Consuegra E 34 B4

Corconte E 5 F2
Cordes F 9 F2
Córdoba E 33 D1
Corella E 15 D2
Coria E 22 B3
Cornellana E 4 B3
Corral de Almaguer E 34 C4
Corralejo E 43 d2
Cortegana E 31 F2
Cortes E 15 E1
Coruche P 20 C2
Costa da Caparica P 20 B1
Costa Nova P 10 B2
Couiza F 18 A2
Coutras F 8 C4
Covadonga E 5 D3
Covaleda E 14 B2
Covarrubias E 14 A2
Covilhã P 21 F4
Crato P 21 E2
Créon F 8 B4
Cressensac F 9 F4
Crevillente E 42 C3
Cruzamento de Pegões P 20 C1
Cruzy F 18 C2
Cuba P 31 D3
Cudillero E 4 B4
Cuéllar E 13 E1
Cuenca E 25 E1
Cuerva E 24 A1
Cueva de la Pileta E 39 D2
Cuevas del Almanzora E 41 F2
Cuevas del Becerro E 39 E3
Cúllar de Baza E 41 E3
Cullera E 36 C2
Cuntis E 2 B2
Curia P 10 B1

D

Daimiel E 34 B3
Daroca E 26 B3
Dax F 7 F2
Dehesa de Campoamor E 42 C3
Denia E 36 C1
Deva E 6 C2
Dolores E 42 C3
Domme F 9 E3
Don Benito E 32 C4
Doña Mencía E 40 A4
Donostia/San Sebastián E 7 D1
Donzenac F 9 F4
Donzère F 19 F4
Dos Hermanas E 38 C4
Dueñas E 13 E2
Durango E 6 C1
Duras F 8 C3
Durban-Corbières F 18 B2
Dúrcal E 40 B2

E

Eaux-Bonnes F 16 B3
Eaux-Chaudes F 16 B3
Eauze F 8 C2
Echarri/Aranaz E 15 D3
Écija E 39 E4
Eibar E 6 C1
Eivissa/Ibiza E 44 A3
Ejea de los Caballeros E 15 F1
El Arahal E 39 D4
El Barco de Avila E 23 D3

El Berrón E	4	C3
El Bodón E	22	B4
El Bonillo E	35	D2
El Bosque E	39	D3
El Burgo E	39	E2
El Burgo de Ebro E	26	C3
El Burgo de Osma E	14	B1
El Cabaco E	22	C4
El Cubo de Tierra del Vino E	12	B1
El Escorial E	24	B3
El Grado E	16	C1
El Masnou E	28	C2
El Molar E	24	C3
El Pardo E	24	B2
El Pedroso E	32	B1
El Perelló E	36	C2
El Perelló E	27	E1
El Pla de Sta María E	28	A2
El Pont de Suert E	17	D1
El Port de la Selva E	29	E4
El Portil E	31	E1
El Prat del Llobregat E	28	C2
El Puente del Arzobispo E	23	E2
El Puerto de Santa Maria E	38	B3
El Real de San Vicente E	23	F2
El Rocío E	38	B4
El Ronquillo E	32	B1
El Saler E	36	C2
El Saucejo E	39	E3
El Serrat AND	17	E1
El Tejar E	39	F3
El Toboso E	34	C3
El Vendrell E	28	B2
El Villar de Arnedo E	15	D2
Elantxobe E	6	C2
Elche E	42	C3
Elche de la Sierra E	35	D1
Elda E	42	C4
Elgoibar E	6	C1
Elizondo E	15	F4
Elne F	18	B1
Elvas P	31	F4
Empúriabrava E	29	E4
Encamp AND	17	E1
Encinasola E	31	F3
Enfesta/Pontecesures E	2	B2
Enguera E	36	B2
Entronoamento P	21	D3
Épila E	26	B4
Ericeira P	20	B2
Errazu E	15	F4
Erro E	15	E3
Ervidel P	30	C3
Es Cana E	44	B3
Escalada E	14	A4
Escalona E	23	F2
Escároz E	15	F3
Escatrón E	27	D3
Escombreras E	42	B2
Espejo E	40	A4
Espelette F	7	E1
Espiel E	33	D2
Espinama E	5	D2
Espinho P	10	B2
Espinosa de los Monteros E	31	D2
Espíritu Santo P	31	D2
Esposende P	10	B4
Espot E	17	D1
Estarreja P	10	B2
Estella E	15	D3
Estepa E	39	E3
Estepona E	39	D2
Esterri de Aneu E	17	D2
Estoril P	20	A2
Estremoz P	21	E1

Évora P	31	D4
Eymet F	8	C3
Ezcaray E	14	B2

F

Facture F	8	A4
Faial P	45	b2
Falset E	27	E2
Fanjeaux F	18	A2
Faro P	30	C1
Fataca P	30	B2
Fátima P	20	C3
Favareta E	36	C2
Feces de Abajo P	11	E3
Felanitx E	45	D3
Felgueiras P	10	C3
Fene E	3	D4
Feria E	32	A3
Fermoselle E	12	A2
Ferreira do Alentejo E	30	C3
Ferreira do Zêzere P	21	D3
Ferrol E	3	D4
Figeac F	9	F3
Figueira da Foz P	10	A1
Figueira de Castelo Rodrigo P	11	E1
Figueiró dos Vinhos P	21	D3
Figueres E	29	E4
Fisterra E	2	A3
Fitero E	15	D1
Fleurance F	9	D2
Flix E	27	E2
Florac F	19	D4
Foix F	17	F2
Fonsagrada E	3	E2
Font-Romeu F	17	F1
Fontecha E	14	C3
Formentor E	45	D4
Fornalutux E	45	D4
Fornells E	45	F4
Fornos de Algodres P	11	D1
Fortuna E	42	B3
Fos F	17	D2
Fos-sur-Mer F	19	F2
Fourcès F	8	C2
Foz E	3	E3
Foz do Arelho P	20	B3
Fraga E	27	E3
Frayssinet F	9	E3
Fregenal de la Sierra E	32	A3
Freixo de Espada à Cinta P	11	E2
Frómista E	13	E3
Fronsac F	17	D2
Fronteira P	21	E1
Frontera E	42	a1
Frontignan F	19	D2
Fuencaliente E	33	E2
Fuendejalon E	26	B4
Fuengirola E	39	E2
Fuenmayor E	14	C3
Fuente Dé E	5	D2
Fuente de Cantos E	32	B2
Fuente el Fresno E	34	B3
Fuente el Saz E	24	C3
Fuente-Obejuna E	32	C2
Fuenterrabía/Hondarribia F	7	D2
Fuentes E	35	E4
Fuentes de Ayódar E	36	C4
Fuentes de Ebro E	26	C3
Fuentes de Oñoro E	22	B4
Fuentesaúco E	12	C1
Fumel F	9	D3
Funchal P	45	b1
Fundão P	21	F3

Furadouro Praia P	10	B2
Fuzeta P	30	C1

G

Gabarret F	8	B2
Gaillac F	9	F1
Galdar E	43	c1
Galizano E	6	A2
Gallargues F	19	E3
Gallur E	15	E1
Gan F	16	B3
Gandesa E	27	E2
Gandia E	36	C1
Ganges F	19	D3
Garraf E	28	B2
Garray E	14	C1
Garrovillas E	22	B2
Garrucha E	41	F2
Gasteiz/Vitoria E	14	C3
Gaucín E	39	D2
Gavarnie F	16	C2
Gavião P	21	E2
Gelida E	28	B2
Génolhac F	19	E4
Gérgal E	41	D2
Gernika/Lumo E	6	C2
Gerona/Girona E	29	D3
Getafe E	24	B2
Getxo/Algorta E	6	B2
Gibraleón E	31	E1
Gibraltar GBZ	39	D1
Gignac F	19	D3
Gijón E	4	C3
Gimont F	17	E4
Girona/Gerona E	29	D3
Gironella E	28	C3
Góis P	21	E4
Golada E	2	C2
Golegã P	21	D3
Golpejas E	12	B1
Gómara E	25	F4
Gondrin F	8	C2
Gourdon F	9	E3
Grado E	4	B3
Gramat F	9	F3
Gran Tarajal E	43	d1
Granada E	40	B2
Granadilla de Abona E	43	b1
Grandas de Salime E	3	F3
Grândola P	30	C4
Granja P	10	B2
Granollers E	28	C2
Graulhet F	18	A4
Graus E	16	C1
Grazalema E	39	D2
Gredos E	23	E3
Grenade F	8	B2
Grenade F	9	E1
Grignols F	8	C3
Griñón E	24	B2
Grisolles F	9	E1
Gruissan F	18	C2
Guadahortuna E	40	C3
Guadalajara E	24	C2
Guadalcanal E	32	B2
Guadalmina E	39	D2
Guadalupe E	23	D1
Guadarrama E	24	B3
Guadix E	40	C2
Guarda P	22	A4
Guardamar del Segura E	42	C3
Guardo E	5	D2
Guareña E	32	B4

Guarromán E 34 A1
Guetaria E 7 D2
Guethary F 7 E2
Guijuelo E 23 D3
Guimarães P 10 C3
Guincho P 20 A2
Guisamo E 2 C3
Guitiriz E 3 D3
Guîtres F 8 C4
Gujan-Mestras F 8 A4
Gumiel de Hizán E 14 A2
Guntín E 3 D2

H

Hagetmau F 8 A2
Haro E 14 C3
Hasparren F 7 E1
Hellín E 35 E1
Hendaye F 7 D2
Herencia E 34 C3
Herrera de Pisuerga E 13 F4
Herrera del Duque E 33 E4
Herreruela E 22 A2
Híjar E 26 C2
Hinojosa del Duque E 33 D2
Homps F 18 B2
Hondarribia/Fuenterrabía F 7 D2
Honrubia E 35 E3
Hontoria del Pinar E 14 B1
Horcajo de Santiago E 34 C4
Hornos E 41 E4
Hortezuela E 25 D4
Hortigüela E 14 B2
Hossegor F 7 E2
Hostalrich E 29 D3
Hostens F 8 B3
Houeillès F 8 C3
Hoyos E 22 B3
Huelma E 40 C3
Huelva E 31 E1
Huércal-Overa E 41 F2
Huesca E 16 B1
Huéscar E 41 E3
Huete E 25 D1

I

Ibeas de Juarros E 14 B3
Ibi E 43 D4
Ibiza/Eivissa E 44 A3
Iciar E 6 C1
Idanha-a-Nova P 21 F3
Igualada E 28 B3
Illano E 3 F3
Illar E 41 D2
Illescas E 24 B2
Inca E 45 D3
Infiesto E 5 D3
Irun E 7 D1
Iruñea/Pamplona E 15 E3
Irurita E 15 E4
Irurzun E 15 E3
Isaba E 16 A3
Iscar E 13 D1
Isla E 6 A2
Isla Cristina E 31 D1
Isona E 28 A4
Istres F 19 F2
Itxassou F 7 E1
Izeda P 11 F3
Iznájar E 40 A3

Iznalloz E 40 C3

J

Jaca E 16 B2
Jadraque E 25 D3
Jaén E 40 B4
Jandia Playa E 43 d1
Jaraicejo E 22 C2
Jaraiz E 23 D2
Jarandilla E 23 D3
Jávea E 43 E4
Jerez de la Frontera E 38 B3
Jerez de los Caballeros E 31 F3
Jijona E 43 D4
Jimena E 40 C4
Jimena de la Frontera E 39 D2
Jódar E 40 C4
Joyeuse F 19 E4
Juillac F 9 E4
Jumilla E 42 B4
Junqueira P 11 E2

L

L'Albi E 27 F3
L'Alcúdia E 36 B2
L'Alcúdia de Crespins E 36 B1
L'Aldea E 27 E1
L'Ametlla de Mar E 27 E1
L'Ampolla E 27 E1
L'Escala E 29 E3
L'Espluga de Francolí E 27 F2
L'Estartit E 29 E3
L'Hospitalet de l'Infant E 27 F2
L'Isle-de-Noé F 17 D4
L'Isle-en-Dodon F 17 D3
L'Isle-Jourdain F 17 E4
La Alamedilla E 23 F3
La Alberca E 22 C3
La Albuera E 32 A4
La Almarcha E 35 E4
La Almolda E 27 D3
La Almunia de Doña Godina E 26 B3
La Antilla E 31 E1
La Bañeza E 12 C4
La Barrela E 3 D2
La Barrosa E 38 B2
La Bastide de-Sérou F 17 E2
La Bisbal E 29 E3
La Bóveda de Toro E 12 C1
La Cabrera E 24 C3
La Calobra E 45 D4
La Calzada de Calatrava E 34 A2
La Carlota E 39 E4
La Carolina E 34 A1
La Cava E 27 E1
La Cavalerie F 18 C4
La Coruña/A Coruña E 2 C4
La Espina E 4 B3
La Gineta E 35 E2
La Granadella E 27 E2
La Grand-Combe F 19 E4
La Grande-Motte F 19 E3
La Granja E 24 B3
La Guardia E 24 B1
La Hermida E 5 E2
La Iglesuela del Cid E 26 C1
La Isla E 5 D3
La Jonquera E 29 E4
La Laguna E 43 b1
La Línea de la Concepción E 39 D1

La Luisiana E 39 E4
La Magdalena E 4 B2
La Malène F 19 D4
La Manga del Mar Menor E 42 C2
La Molina E 28 C4
La Mongie F 16 C2
La Mudarra E 13 D2
La Muela E 26 B4
La Nava de Ricomalillo E 23 E1
La Oliva E 43 d2
La Paca E 41 F3
La Palma del Condado E 31 F1
La Platja d'Aro E 29 E3
La Pobla de Segur E 17 D1
La Pola de Gordón E 4 C2
La Puebla de Cazalla E 39 D3
La Puebla de Montalbán E 23 F1
La Puebla de Valverde E 36 B4
La Rambla E 39 F4
La Réole F 8 C3
La Robla E 4 C2
La Roca de la Sierra E 22 A1
La Roca del Vallés E 28 C2
La Roda E 35 E3
La Roque-Gageac F 9 E3
La Salvetat F 9 F2
La Salvetat-sur-Agout F 18 B3
La Seu d'Urgell E 17 E1
La Solana E 34 B2
La Unión E 42 B2
La Vecilla E 4 C2
Labastide-d'Armagnac F 8 B2
Labastide-Murat F 9 E3
Labenne F 7 E2
Labouheyre F 8 A3
Labrède F 8 B4
Labrit F 8.–B3
Lacalahorra E 40 C2
Lacapelle-Marival F 9 F3
Lacaune F 18 C3
Lacq F 16 B4
Ladoeiro P 21 F3
Lafrançaise F 9 E2
Lagoa P 30 B1
Lagos P 30 B1
Lagrasse F 18 B2
Laguardia E 14 C3
Laguépie F 9 F2
Lalín E 2 C2
Lalinde F 9 D4
Lamalou-les-Bains F 18 C3
Lamego P 11 D2
Landete E 36 A4
Langoiran F 8 B4
Langon F 8 B3
Lanjarón E 40 B2
Lannemezan F 16 C3
Laplume F 8 C2
Larche F 9 E4
Laredo E 6 B2
Laroque-des-Arcs F 9 E3
Larrau F 16 A3
Laruns F 16 B3
Las Cabezas de San Juan E 38 C3
Las Caldas de Besaya E 5 F2
Las Campanas E 15 E3
Las Navas del Marqués E 24 A3
Las Negras E 41 E1
Las Palmas de Gran Canaria E 43 c1
Las Pedroñeras E 35 D3
Las Rozas E 24 B2
Las Ventas con Peña Aguilera E 23 F1
Laujar de Andarax E 41 D2
Lautrec F 18 B3
Lauzerte F 9 D2
Lauzun F 9 D3

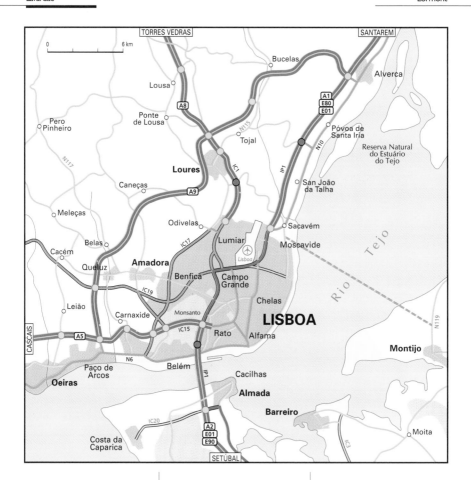

Lavardac F	8	C2
Lavaur F	18	A4
Lavelanet F	17	F2
Lavre P	20	C1
Laxe E	2	B4
Le Barp F	8	A4
Le Boulou F	18	B1
Le Bugue F	9	D4
Le Cap-d'Agde F	19	D2
Le Caylar F	19	D3
Le Fossat F	17	E3
Le Grau-du-Roi F	19	E3
Le Mas-d'Azil F	17	E2
Le Muret F	8	A3
Le Perthus F	29	D4
Le Rozier F	19	D4
Le Teil F	19	F4
Le Vigan F	19	D4
Lebrija E	38	C3
Lécera E	26	C3
Lectoure F	8	C2
Ledesma E	12	B1
Lédignan F	19	E3
Ledigos E	13	E3
Léguevin F	17	E3
Legutiano E	14	C4
Leiria P	20	C3

Lekeitio E	6	C2
Lekunberri E	15	E3
Lembeye F	16	C4
León E	4	C2
Léon F	7	E2
Lepe E	31	E1
Lérida (Lleida) E	27	E3
Lerma E	14	A2
Lés E	17	D2
Les Baux-de-Provence F	19	F3
Les Borges Blanques E	27	F3
Les Cabannes F	17	F2
Les Escaldes AND	17	E1
Les Eyzies-de-Tayac F	9	E4
Les Vans F	19	E4
Lescar F	16	B4
Lestelle Bétharram F	16	B3
Leucate F	18	C2
Leyre F	15	F2
Lézignan-Corbières F	18	B2
Libourne F	8	C4
Lillo E	34	C4
Limogne-en-Quercy F	9	F2
Limoux F	18	A2
Linares E	34	A1
Linares de Riofrío E	23	D4
Lindoso P	11	D4

Liria E	36	B3
Lisboa P	20	B2
Lisle F	9	E1
Lit-et-Mixe F	7	F3
Livernon F	9	F3
Llafranc E	29	E3
Llagostera E	29	D3
Llançà E	29	E4
Llanes E	5	E3
Llavorsi E	17	E1
Lleida (Lérida) E	27	E3
Llerena E	32	B2
Lles E	17	E1
Llodio E	6	B2
Lloret de Mar E	29	D3
Llucmayor E	45	D3
Lodève F	19	D3
Lodosa E	15	D2
Loeches E	24	C2
Logroño E	14	C2
Logrosán E	23	D1
Loja E	40	A3
Lombez F	17	E3
Lopera E	33	E1
Lora del Río E	32	C1
Lorca E	42	A3
Lormont F	8	B4

Los Alcázares E 42 C2
Los Arcos E 15 D3
Los Arenales del Sol E 43 D3
Los Barrios E 38 C1
Los Cristianos E 43 b1
Los Llanos de Aridane E 42 a2
Los Navalmorales E 23 E1
Los Palacios y Villafranca E 38 C3
Los Urrutias E 42 C2
Losar de la Vera E 23 D3
Loulé P 30 C1
Lourdes F 16 C3
Louredo P 11 D3
Lourinha P 20 B3
Lousã P 21 D4
Lousada P 10 C3
Lovios E 11 D4
Lozoyuela E 24 C3
Luanco E 4 C4
Luarca E 4 B4
Lubia E 14 C1
Lucena E 39 F3
Lucena del Cid E 36 C4
Luciana E 33 F3
Lugo E 3 D2
Lugones E 4 C3
Lumbier E 15 F2

Lumbrales E 11 F1
Lumo/Gernika E 6 C2
Lunas F 18 C3
Lunel F 19 E3
Luso P 10 B1
Lussan F 19 F4
Luz-St-Sauveur F 16 C2

M

Maçanet de la Selva E 29 D3
Mação P 21 E3
Macedo de Cavaleiros P 11 F3
Machico P 45 b1
Madrid E 24 B2
Madridejos E 34 B4
Madrigal de las Altas Torres E .. 23 F4
Maella E 27 D2
Mafra P 20 B2
Magallón E 15 E1
Magaluf E 44 C3
Magaz E 13 E2
Magescq F 7 F2
Mahón E 45 F3
Mahora E 35 E2

Maials E 27 E3
Málaga E 39 F2
Malagón E 34 B3
Malpartida de Cáceres E 22 B2
Malpica E 2 B4
Manacor E 45 D3
Mancha Real E 40 C4
Mangualde P 10 C1
Manresa E 28 B3
Mansilla de las Mulas E 4 C1
Manteigas P 21 F4
Manzanares E 34 B3
Manzanares el Real E 24 B3
Maqueda E 23 F2
Maranchón E 25 E3
Marateca P 20 C1
Marbella E 39 E2
Marchena E 39 D4
Marcheprime F 8 A4
Marciac F 16 C4
Marcilla E 15 E2
Marín E 2 B2
Marinha Grande P 20 C3
Marmande F 8 C3
Marseillan F 19 D2
Marseillan-Plage F 19 D2
Martel F 9 F4

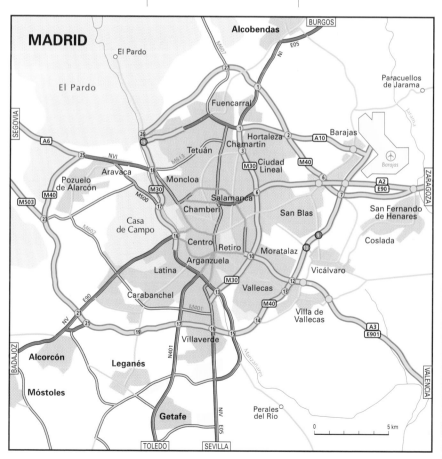

Martigues F	19	F2
Martín de Yeltes E	22	C4
Martorell E	28	B2
Martos E	40	B4
Marvão P	21	F2
Masegoso de Tajuña E	25	D3
Maspalomas E	43	c1
Massat F	17	E2
Masseube F	17	D3
Matabuena E	24	C4
Matalascañas E	38	B3
Matalebreras E	15	D1
Matallana E	13	D3
Mataró E	28	C2
Matos de Carrico P	20	C4
Matosinhos P	10	B3
Maubourguet F	16	C4
Mauléon-Licharre F	16	A3
Maury F	18	B1
Mauvezin F	9	D1
Mayorga E	13	D3
Mazagón E	38	B4
Mazamet F	18	B3
Mazarrón E	42	B2
Mazères F	17	F3
Mazo E	42	a2
Mealhada P	10	B1
Medellin E	32	C4
Medina de Rioseco E	13	D2
Medina del Campo E	13	D1
Medina-Sidonia E	38	C2
Medinaceli E	25	E3
Meira E	3	E3
Melgaço P	2	B1
Melide E	3	D2
Melides P	30	B4
Mendavia E	15	D2
Mengibar E	40	B4
Mequinenza E	27	E3
Mera E	3	D4
Mercadal E	45	E4
Mérida E	32	B4
Mértola P	31	D2
Mesão Frio P	11	D2
Mesón do Vento E	2	C3
Meyrueis F	19	D4
Mèze F	19	D2
Mézin F	8	C2
Miajadas E	32	C4
Miami Platja E	27	F2
Miélan E	17	D3
Mieres E	4	C3
Mijas E	39	E2
Millas F	18	B1
Millau F	18	C4
Mimizan F	7	F3
Mimizan-Plage F	7	F3
Minglanilla E	35	F3
Mira E	36	A3
Mira P	10	B1
Miraflores de la Sierra E	24	B3
Miramar P	10	B3
Miramas E	19	F2
Miramont-de-Guyenne F	8	C3
Miranda de Ebro E	14	C3
Miranda do Douro P	12	A2
Mirande F	17	D4
Mirandela P	11	E3
Mirantes E	4	B2
Miravalles E	6	B2
Miravet E	27	E2
Mirepoix F	17	F2
Moaña E	2	B2
Mogadouro P	11	F2
Mogón E	41	D4
Moguer E	31	E1

Moiá E	28	C3
Moimenta da Beira P	11	D2
Moissac F	9	D2
Moita P	20	B1
Mojácar E	41	F2
Moledo P	10	C4
Molières F	9	E2
Molina de Aragón E	25	F2
Molins de Rei E	28	C2
Mollerusa E	27	F3
Mollet E	28	C2
Mombeltrán E	23	E3
Monachil E	40	B2
Monção P	2	B1
Monchique P	30	B2
Moncófar E	36	C3
Mondariz Balneario E	2	B1
Mondim de Basto P	11	D3
Mondoñedo E	3	E3
Mondragón E	15	D4
Monesterio E	32	B2
Monflanquin F	9	D3
Monforte P	21	E1
Monforte de Lemos E	3	D1
Monóvar E	42	C4
Monpazier F	9	D3
Monreal E	15	E3
Monreal del Campo E	26	A2
Monroyo E	27	D2
Monségur F	8	C3
Mont-de-Marsan F	8	B2
Mont-Louis F	18	A1
Montagnac F	19	D3
Montaigu-de-Quercy F	9	D3
Montalbán E	26	B2
Montamarta E	12	B2
Montañana E	26	C4
Montánchez E	22	B1
Montaren E	19	E4
Montargil P	21	D2
Montastruc la-Conseillère F	17	F4
Montauban F	9	E2
Montbazens F	9	F2
Montblanc E	28	A2
Montcuq F	9	E2
Monte Clérigo P	30	B2
Monte Gordo P	31	D1
Montealagre del Castillo E	35	F1
Montefrío E	40	B3
Montehermoso E	22	C3
Montélimar F	19	F4
Montemor-o-Novo P	20	C1
Montemor-o-Velho P	21	D4
Monterroso E	3	D2
Montesquieu-Volvestre F	17	E3
Montesquiou F	17	D4
Montfort F	7	F2
Montgat E	28	C2
Montgiscard F	17	F3
Montignac F	9	E4
Montijo E	32	B4
Montijo P	20	B1
Montilla E	39	F4
Montorio E	14	A3
Montoro E	33	E1
Montpellier F	19	D3
Montpezat F	9	E2
Montpon-Ménestérol F	8	C4
Montréal E	8	C2
Montréal F	18	A2
Montréjeau F	17	D3
Montseny E	28	C3
Monzón E	27	E4
Mora E	34	B4
Mora P	21	D1
Móra d'Ebre E	27	E2

Mora de Rubielos E	36	C4
Móra la Nova E	27	E2
Moraira E	43	E4
Morasverdes E	22	C4
Moratalla E	42	A4
Morcenx F	8	A3
Moreda E	40	C3
Morella E	27	D1
Morlaàs F	16	B3
Morón de Almazán E	25	E4
Morón de la Frontera E	39	D3
Mota del Cuervo E	35	D3
Mota del Marques E	13	D2
Motilla del Palancar E	35	E3
Motril E	40	B2
Moura P	31	E3
Mourão P	31	E3
Mouthoumet F	18	B2
Muelas del Pan E	12	B2
Mugron F	8	A2
Mula E	42	B3
Munera E	35	D2
Mungia E	6	C2
Muñico E	23	E3
Muniesa E	26	C2
Muranzel P	10	B2
Murat-sur-Vèbre F	18	C3
Murça P	11	E3
Murcia E	42	B3
Muret F	17	E3
Murguia E	14	C4
Muros E	2	B3
Murtosa P	10	B2
Muskiz E	6	B2
Mussidan F	9	D4
Mutrico E	6	C2

N

Nadela E	3	D2
Nailloux F	17	F3
Najac F	9	F2
Nájera E	14	C3
Nalzen F	17	F2
Nanclares de Oca E	14	C3
Nant F	19	D4
Narbonne F	18	C2
Narbonne-Plage F	18	C2
Nava E	4	C3
Nava de la Asunción E	24	A4
Nava del Rey E	12	C1
Navacerrada E	24	B3
Navahermosa E	23	F1
Navalcarnero E	24	B2
Navalmanzano E	24	B4
Navalmoral de la Mata E	23	D2
Navalperal E	24	A3
Navarrenx F	16	B4
Navarrete E	14	C2
Navas de San Juan E	34	B1
Navas del Rey E	24	A2
Navatalgordo E	23	F3
Navia E	4	A4
Nazare P	20	C3
Neauvic F	9	D4
Neda E	3	D4
Nelas P	10	C1
Nérac F	8	C2
Nerja E	40	B2
Niebla E	31	F1
Nijar E	41	E1
Nîmes F	19	E3
Nisa P	21	E2
Noain E	15	E3

Nogaro F 8 B2
Noia E 2 B3
Noja E 6 A2
Novelda E 42 C4
Noves F 19 F3
Nuévalos E 26 A3
Nules E 36 C3

O

O Barco de Valdeorras E 3 E1
O Cádabo/Baleira E 3 E2
O Grove E 2 B2
Óbidos P 20 B3
Ocaña E 24 B1
Ochagavia E 15 F3
Odeceixe P 30 B2
Odeleite P 31 D1
Odemira P 30 B2
Ofir P 10 B3
Oia (Arrabal) E 2 A1
Ojén E 39 E2
Olargues F 18 C3
Olazagutiá E 15 D3
Oleiros E 2 B2
Oleiros P 21 E3
Olette F 18 A1
Olhão P 30 C1
Olite E 15 E2
Oliva E 36 C1
Olivares de Júcar E 35 E4
Oliveira de Azeméis P 10 B2
Oliveira de Frades P 10 C2
Oliveira do Bairro P 10 B1
Oliveira do Hospital P 21 E4
Olivenza E 31 F4
Olmedillo de Roa E 13 F2
Olmedo E 13 D1
Olmillos de Sasamón E 13 F3
Olonzac F 18 B2
Oloron-Ste-Marie F 16 B3
Olot E 29 D4
Olvega E 15 D1
Olvera E 39 D3
Oña E 14 B3
Onda E 36 C3
Ondara E 36 C1
Ontinyent E 36 B1
Ontur E 35 F1
Orange F 19 F4
Orcera E 34 C1
Ordes E 2 C3
Ordino AND 17 E1
Orduña E 6 B1
Orense/Ourense E 2 C1
Orgaz E 34 B4
Orihuela E 42 C3
Orihuela del Tremedal E 25 F2
Orio E 7 D1
Órjiva E 40 C2
Orol E 3 E4
Oropesa E 23 E2
Oropesa del Mar E 37 D3
Orthez F 7 F1
Ortigueira E 3 D4
Oseja de Sajambre E 5 D2
Osera E 26 C3
Osorno E 13 E3
Ossa de Montiel E 34 C2
Ostiz E 15 E3
Osuna E 39 E3
Otero de Bodas E 12 B3
Ourense/Orense E 2 C1
Ourique P 30 C2

Oust F 17 E2
Ovar P 10 B2
Oviedo E 4 C3

P

Padron E 2 B2
Padul E 40 B2
Paguera E 44 C3
Palacios de Sanabria E 12 A3
Palacios del Sil E 4 A2
Palafrugell E 29 E3
Palamós E 29 E3
Palas de Rei E 3 D2
Palavas-les-Flots F 19 E3
Palencia E 13 E2
Palheiros de Mira P 10 B1
Palheiros de Quiaios P 10 A1
Palheiros de Tocha P 10 A1
Palma E 44 C3
Palma del Río E 32 C1
Palma Nova E 44 C3
Palmela P 20 B1
Palomares E 41 F2
Pamiers F 17 F2
Pampilhosa da Serra P 21 E3
Pamplona/Iruñea E 15 E3
Panassac F 17 D3
Pancorvo E 14 B3
Panes E 5 E3
Panxon E 2 B1
Paredes P 10 C3
Paredes de Nava E 13 E3
Parentis-en-Born F 7 F3
Pas de la Casa AND 17 F1
Pasaia E 7 D1
Pastrana E 25 D2
Pau F 16 B3
Pavia P 21 D1
Payrac F 9 E3

Peal de Becerro E 41 D4
Pedras Salgadas P 11 D3
Pedraza E 24 C4
Pedro Muñoz E 34 C3
Pego E 36 C1
Peidralaves E 23 F2
Pellegrue F 8 C4
Penacova P 21 E4
Penafiel E 13 E1
Penafiel P 10 C3
Penamacor P 22 A3
Penaranda E 14 A1
Peñaranda de Bracamonte E 23 E4
Peñarroya-Pueblonuevo E 33 D2
Penas de S Pedro E 35 E1
Penela E 21 D4
Peniche P 20 B3
Peñíscola E 37 E4
Peralejos de las Truchas E 25 F2
Perales del Alfambra E 26 B2
Peralta E 15 E2
Pereiro P 31 D2
Périgueux F 9 D4
Perpignan F 18 B1
Petrá E 45 D3
Peyrehorade F 7 F2
Pézenas F 19 D3
Pias P 31 E3
Picacho de Veleta E 40 C2
Piedrabuena E 33 F3
Piedrafita de Babia E 4 B3
Piedrahita E 23 E3
Pierrefitte-Nestalas F 16 C3
Pierrelatte F 19 F4
Pierroton F 8 B4
Pilat-Plage F 7 F4
Pina de Ebro E 26 C3
Pineda de Mar E 29 D2
Pinhel P 11 E1
Pinos Puente E 40 B3
Pinoso E 42 C4
Pissos F 8 A3

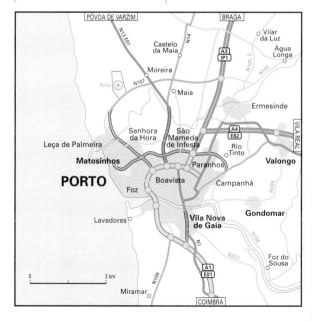

Plaisance F	8	B1
Plasencia E	22	C3
Playa Blanca E	43	d2
Playa de las Americas E	43	b1
Playa de San Juán E	43	D4
Plentzia E	6	B2
Pobes E	14	C3
Podensac F	8	B4
Pola de Allande E	4	A3
Pola de Laviana E	4	C3
Pola de Lena E	4	C3
Pola de Siero E	4	C3
Pola de Somiedo E	4	B3
Pola de Trives E	3	D1
Pollença E	45	D4
Pombal P	21	D4
Ponferrada E	3	F1
Pont-de-Salars F	18	C4
Pont-St-Esprit F	19	F4
Ponta do Sol P	45	a1
Pontacq F	16	C3
Pontão P	21	D3
Ponte Barxas E	2	C1
Ponte Caldelas E	2	B2
Ponte da Barca P	10	C4
Ponte de Lima P	10	C4
Ponte de Sor P	21	D2
Ponteareas E	2	B1
Pontecesures/Enfesta E	2	B2
Pontedeume E	3	D4
Pontevedra E	2	B2
Ponts E	28	A3
Porcuna E	40	B4
Porriño E	2	B1
Port-Barcarès F	18	C1
Port-Camargue F	19	E2
Port-de-Bouc F	19	F2
Port-Leucate F	18	C1
Port-la-Nouvelle F	18	C2
Port-St-Louis-du-Rhône F	19	F2
Port-Ste-Marie F	8	C3
Port-Vendres F	29	E4
Portalegre P	21	E2
Portalrubio E	26	B2
Portbou E	29	E4
Portel P	31	D3
Portela de Messines P	30	C1
Portela do Homem E	11	D4
Portelo P	12	A3
Portimão P	30	B1
Portinatx E	44	B3
Porto P	10	B3
Porto Cristo E	45	D3
Porto de Mós P	20	C3
Porto do Son E	2	B3
Porto Moniz P	45	a2
Portomarín E	3	D2
Portomouro E	2	C3
Porzuna E	34	A3
Posadas E	33	D1
Potes E	5	E2
Pouyastruc F	16	C3
Póvoa de Lanhoso P	10	C3
Póvoa de Varzim P	10	B3
Pozo Alcón E	41	D3
Pozoblanco E	33	D2
Pozuelo de Ariza E	25	F4
Pozuelo de Zarzón E	22	C3
Prades F	18	A1
Pradillo E	14	C2
Praia da Rocha P	30	B1
Praia de Santa Cruz P	20	B2
Praia Grande P	20	A2
Prats de Llucanés E	28	C3
Prats-de-Mollo-la-Preste F	29	D4
Pravia E	4	B4

Premiá de Mar E	28	C2
Priego E	25	E2
Priego de Córdoba E	40	A3
Proença-a-Nova P	21	E3
Puçol E	36	C3
Puebla de Alcocer E	33	D3
Puebla de Don Fadrique E	41	E4
Puebla de Don Rodrigo E	33	E3
Puebla de Lillo E	4	C2
Puebla de Obando E	22	A1
Puebla de Sanabria E	12	A3
Puebla Tornesa E	37	D4
Puente la Reina E	15	E3
Puente Viesgo E	5	F2
Puente-Genil E	39	F3
Puentelarra E	14	C3
Puerto Banús E	39	E2
Puerto Castilla E	23	D3
Puerto de Alcúdia E	45	D4
Puerto de Andraitx E	44	C3
Puerto de la Cruz E	43	b1
Puerto de Mazarrón E	42	B2
Puerto de Pollença E	45	D4
Puerto de San Vicente E	23	D1
Puerto de Sóller E	45	D4
Puerto del Carmen E	43	d2
Puerto del Rosario E	43	d1
Puerto Lápice E	34	B3
Puerto Lastres E	5	D3
Puerto Real E	38	B2
Puerto Rico E	43	c1
Puerto-Lumbreras E	41	F2
Puertollano E	33	F2
Puigcerda E	17	F1
Puivert F	18	A2
Punta Umbría E	38	A4
Puntagorda E	42	a2
Purchena E	41	E2
Puy-l'Evêque F	9	E3
Puylaurens F	18	A3
Pyla-sur-Mer F	7	F4

Q

Quarteira P	30	C1
Quesada E	41	D4
Quillan F	18	A2
Quintana de la Serena E	32	C3
Quintana del Puente E	13	E2
Quintanaortuño E	14	A3
Quintanar de la Orden E	34	C4
Quintanar de la Sierra E	14	B2
Quintanilha P	12	A3
Quinto E	26	C3
Quiroga E	3	D1
Quissac F	19	E3

R

Rábade E	3	D3
Rabastens F	9	E1
Rabastens-de-Bigorre F	16	C3
Ramacastañas E	23	E2
Ramales de la Victoria E	6	A2
Rascafría E	24	B3
Réalmont F	18	B4
Rebordelo P	11	E3
Redondela E	2	B2
Redondo E	31	E4
Regua P	11	D2
Reguengos de Monsaraz P	31	E3
Reinosa E	5	E2

Remoulins F	19	F3
Rentería E	7	D1
Requena E	36	A3
Réquista F	18	B4
Retama E	33	F3
Reus E	27	F2
Revel F	18	A3
Riaño E	5	D2
Riaza E	24	C4
Riba de Aire P	10	C3
Ribadavia E	2	C1
Ribadelago E	12	A4
Ribadeo E	3	F3
Ribadesella E	5	D3
Ribeira Brava P	45	a1
Ribera (Santa Eugenia) E	2	B2
Ribes de Freser E	28	C4
Ricla E	26	B4
Rieumes F	17	E3
Rieupeyroux F	9	F2
Rieux F	17	E3
Rincón de la Victoria E	39	F2
Rio de Mouro P	20	B2
Rio Maior P	20	C3
Riomar E	27	E1
Riopar E	35	D1
Riotinto E	31	F2
Ripoll E	28	C4
Riscle F	8	B2
Rivesaltes F	18	B1
Roa E	13	F1
Robledo de Chavela E	24	A3
Rocamadour F	9	F3
Rodrigatos E	4	B2
Rogil P	30	B2
Roncal E	16	A3
Roncesvalles E	15	F3
Ronda E	39	D2
Roquefort F	8	B2
Roquefort-sur-Soulzon F	18	C4
Roquetas de Mar E	41	D1
Rosal de la Frontera E	31	E2
Roses E	29	E4
Rostassac F	9	E3
Rota E	38	B3
Roujan F	18	C3
Rubena E	14	A3
Rubielos de Mora E	36	C4
Ruidera E	34	C2
Rute E	40	A3

S

S Luis P	30	B3
S Marcos de Ataboeira P	31	D2
S'Agaró E	29	E3
S'Algar E	45	F3
S'Arenal E	44	C3
Sabadell E	28	C2
Sabiñánigo E	16	B2
Sabres F	8	A3
Sabrosa E	11	D2
Sabugal P	22	A4
Sacedón E	25	D2
Sadaba E	15	E2
Sagres P	30	A1
Sagunto E	36	C3
Sahagún E	13	D3
Saillagouse F	17	F1
St-Affrique F	18	C4
St-Ambroix F	19	E4
St-André-de-Cubzac F	8	B4
St-Antonin-Noble-Val F	9	E2
St-Béat F	17	D2

St-Beauzély *F* 18 C4
St-Bertrand-de-Comminges *F* 17 D3
St-Céré *F* 9 F3
St-Chamas *F* 19 F2
St-Chinian *F* 18 C3
St-Clar *F* 9 D2
St-Cyprien *F* 9 E4
St-Cyprien-Plage *F* 18 C1
St-Emilion *F* 8 C4
St-Etienne-de-Baïgorry *F* 15 F4
St-Gaudens *F* 17 D3
St-Geours-de-Maremne *F* 7 E2
St-Gervais *F* 18 C3
St-Géry *F* 9 E3
St-Gilles *F* 19 E3
St-Girons *F* 17 E2
St-Girons-Plage *F* 7 E3
St-Hippolyte-du-Fort *F* 19 E3
St-Jean-de-Luz *F* 7 E2
St-Jean-du-Bruel *F* 19 D4
St-Jean-du-Gard *F* 19 E4
St-Jean-Pied-de-Port *F* 15 F3
St-Jory *F* 17 F4
St-Julien *F* 17 E3
St-Justin *F* 8 B2
St-Lary-Soulan *F* 16 C2
St-Lys *F* 17 E3
St-Macaire *F* 8 B3
St-Martin-de-Londres *F* 19 D3
St-Martory *F* 17 D3
St Miguel de Balansot *E* 44 A3
St-Palais *F* 16 A4
St-Paul-Cap-de-Joux *F* 18 A3
St-Paul-de-Fenouillet *F* 18 B2
St-Pé *F* 16 C3
St-Pierre-de-Chignac *F* 9 D4
St-Pons *F* 18 C3
St-Rémy-de-Provence *F* 19 F3
St-Rome-de-Tarn *F* 18 C4
St-Sernin-sur-Rance *F* 18 B4
St-Sever *F* 8 A2
St-Symphorien *F* 8 B3
St-Vincent-de-Tyrosse *F* 7 E2
Ste-Croix-Volvestre *F* 17 E3
Ste-Enimie *F* 19 D4
Ste-Foy-la-Grande *F* 8 C4
Ste-Hélène *F* 8 A4
Ste-Marie-de-Campan *F* 16 C3
Saissac *F* 18 A3
Salamanca *E* 12 B1
Salardú *E* 17 D2
Salas *E* 4 B3
Salas de los Infantes *E* 14 B2
Saldaña *E* 13 E4
Salema *P* 30 A1
Salies-de-Béarn *F* 7 F1
Salies-du-Salat *F* 17 D3
Salignac-Eyvigues *F* 9 E4
Salinas *E* 4 C4
Sallent de Gállego *E* 16 B2
Salles *F* 8 A4
Salles *F* 17 F3
Salles-Curan *F* 18 C4
Salobreña *E* 40 B2
Salou *E* 27 F2
Salses-le-Château *F* 18 C1
Salvaterra de Magos *P* 20 C2
Salvaterra de Miño *E* 2 B1
Salvatierra *E* 15 D3
Salviac *F* 9 E3
Sama de Langreo *E* 4 C3
Samadet *F* 8 A2
Samatan *F* 17 E3
Samitier *E* 16 C1
Samos *E* 3 E2
San Anton Leitza *E* 15 E4

San Antonio Abad *E* 44 A3
San Bartolomé de la Torre *E* 31 E1
San Clemente *E* 35 D3
San Cosme/Barreiros *E* 3 E3
San Emiliano *E* 4 B2
San Esteban de Gormaz *E* 14 B1
San Fernando *E* 38 B2
San Javier *E* 42 C3
San José *E* 41 E1
San Juán de Alicante *E* 43 D4
San Juan del Puerto *E* 31 E1
San Leonardo de Yagüe *E* 14 B1
San Martín de Unx *E* 15 E2
San Martín de Valdeiglesias *E* 24 A2
San Martín del Pedroso *E* 12 A3
San Mateo *E* 27 D1
San Miguel de Bernúy *E* 13 E1
San Miguel de las Dueñas *E* 3 F1
San Millán de la Cogolla *E* 14 C2
San Nicolás de Tolentino *E* 43 c1
San Pedro de Alcántara *E* 39 D2
San Pedro del Arroyo *E* 23 F3
San Pedro del Pinatar *E* 42 C3
San Pedro do Sul *P* 10 C2
San Rafael *E* 24 B3
San Roque *E* 39 D1
San Sebastian de la Gomera *E* 42 a1
San Sebastián/Donostia *E* 7 D1
San Vincente de la Barquera *E* 5 E3
Sanchidrián *E* 24 A4
Sancti Spiritus *E* 22 C4
Sangüesa *E* 15 F2
Sanguinet *F* 8 A4
Sanlúcar de Barrameda *E* 38 B3
Sanlúcar la Mayor *E* 38 C4
Sant Carles de la Rápita *E* 27 E1
Sant Celoni *E* 28 C3
Sant Feliu de Guixols *E* 29 E3
Sant Francesc de
    Formentera *E* 44 A2
Sant Hilari Sacalm *E* 29 D3
Sant Joan de Labritja *E* 44 B3

Sant Josep de sa Telaia *E* 44 A3
Sant Juliá de Lória *AND* 17 E1
Sant Kurutze Kampezu *E* 15 D3
Sant Pere Pescador *E* 29 E3
Sant Pol de Mar *E* 29 D2
Sant Quirze de Besora *E* 28 C3
Sant Sadurni d'Anoia *E* 28 B2
Santa Bárbara *E* 31 E2
Santa Clara-a-Velha *P* 30 B2
Santa Coloma de Farners *E* 29 D3
Santa Coloma de Queralt *E* 28 A3
Santa Cristina d'Aro *E* 29 D3
Santa Cruz *P* 45 b1
Santa Cruz de la Palma *E* 42 a2
Santa Cruz de Moya *E* 36 A4
Santa Cruz de Mudela *E* 34 B2
Santa Cruz de Tenerife *E* 43 b1
Santa Elena *E* 34 B1
Santa Eufemia *E* 33 D2
Santa Eugenia (Ribera) *E* 2 B2
Santa Eulalia *E* 26 A2
Santa Galdana *E* 45 E4
Santa Joan de les Abadesses *E* 28 C4
Santa María *E* 45 D3
Santa Maria de Huerta *E* 25 F3
Santa Marta *E* 32 A3
Santa Olalla del Cala *E* 32 B2
Santa Pola *E* 42 C3
Santa Susana *E* 29 D2
Sta Comba *E* 2 B3
Sta Comba Dão *P* 10 C1
Sta Eulária d'es Riu *E* 44 B3
Sta María del Campo *E* 13 F2
Sta María del Páramo *E* 12 C4
Sta María la Real de Nieva *E* 24 A4
Santafé *E* 40 B2
Santana *P* 45 b2
Santana de Serra *P* 30 C2
Santander *E* 6 A2
Santanyi *E* 45 D3
Santarém *P* 20 C2
Santed *E* 26 A3

SAN SEBASTIÁN/
DONOSTIA

Santesteban E 15 E4
Santiago de Compostela E ... 2 C3
Santiago de la Ribera E 42 C3
Santiago do Cacém P 30 B3
Santillana del Mar E 5 F2
Santesteban del Puerto E 34 B1
Santo Tirso P 10 C3
Sto Domingo de la Calzada E 14 C3
Sto Domingo de Silos E 14 A2
Santoña E 6 B2
Santurtzi E 6 B2
Sanxenxo E 2 B2
São Bartolomeu de Messines P 30 C2
São Brás de Alportel P 30 C1
São Domingos P 30 C3
São Gregório P 2 C1
São João da Madeira P 10 B2
São João da Pesqueira P 11 D2
São Marcos da Serra P 30 B2
São Martinho do Porto P 20 B3
São Martinhoe P 21 E4
São Pedro de Muel P 20 C4
São Vicente P 45 a2
Saqués E 16 B2
Saramon F 17 D4
Sariñena E 27 D4
Sarlat-la-Canéda F 9 E4
Sarracin E 14 A3
Sarria E 3 D2
Sarrión E 36 B4
Sarron F 8 B1
Satão P 11 D1
Saucats F 8 B4
Sauve F 19 E3
Sauveterre-de-Béarn F 7 F1
Sauveterre-de-Guyenne F 8 C4
Saverdun F 17 F3
Savignac-les-Eglises F 9 E4
Segorbe E 36 C3
Segovia E 24 B4
Segura E 34 C1
Segura P 22 A3

Segura de León E 32 A2
Segura de los Baños E 26 B2
Seia P 21 F4
Seilhac F 9 F4
Seira E 16 C1
Semblana P 30 C2
Sepúlveda E 24 C4
Sequeros E 22 C4
Serém P 10 B2
Serón E 41 E2
Serós E 27 E3
Serpa P 31 D3
Sertã P 21 E3
Sesimbra P 20 B1
Sesma E 15 D2
Sète F 19 D2
Setúbal P 20 B1
Sever P 10 C2
Sévérac-le-Château F 18 C4
Sevilla E 38 C4
Sevilleja de la Jara E 23 E1
Seyches F 8 C3
Sigean F 18 C2
Sigüeiro E 2 C3
Sigüenza E 25 E3
Silla E 36 C2
Silleda E 2 C2
Sils E 29 D3
Silves P 30 B1
Simancas E 13 D2
Sines P 30 B3
Sintra P 20 B2
Siorac-en-Périgord F 9 E4
Sisante E 35 E3
Sitges E 28 B2
Sobrada (Castelo de Paiva) P ... 10 C2
Sobral de Mònte Agraço P 20 B2
Socovos E 41 F4
Solares E 6 A2
Soldeu AND 17 E1
Sóller E 45 D4
Solosancho E 23 E3

Solsona E 28 B4
Solynieve E 40 C2
Sommières F 19 E3
Somosierra E 24 C4
Soncillo E 5 F1
Sonseca E 24 A1
Sopeira E 17 D1
Sorbas E 41 E2
Sore F 8 B3
Soria E 14 C1
Sort E 17 D1
Sos del Rey Católico E 15 F2
Soses E 27 E3
Sotillo de la Adrada E 23 F2
Soto el Real E 24 B3
Sotogrande E 39 D1
Souillac F 9 E4
Soumoulou F 16 C3
Soure P 21 D4
Sousceyrac F 9 F3
Sousel P 21 E1
Soustons F 7 E2
Soutelo E 2 C2
Stes-Maries-de-la-Mer F 19 E2
Suances E 5 F3
Sueca E 36 C2
Súria E 28 B3

T

Tábara E 12 B3
Tabernas E 41 E2
Tabernes E 36 C2
Taboada E 3 D2
Tábua P 21 E4
Tabuaço P 11 D2
Tafalla E 15 E2
Talavera de la Reina E 23 E2
Talayuelas E 36 A4
Tamames E 22 C4
Tamarinda E 45 E4
Tamarite de Litera E 27 E4
Tanger E 38 B1
Tapia de Casariego E 3 F3
Tarajalejo E 43 d1
Tarancón E 24 C1
Tarascon F 19 F3
Tarascon-sur-Ariège F 17 E2
Tarazona E 15 D1
Tarazona de la Mancha E 35 E3
Tarbes F 16 C3
Tardets-Sorholus F 16 A3
Tarifa E 38 C1
Tarnos F 7 E2
Tarragona E 28 A2
Tàrrega E 28 A3
Tartas F 8 A2
Tauste E 15 E1
Tavira P 31 D1
Teguise E 43 d2
Telde E 43 c1
Telheira P 30 B2
Tembleque E 34 B4
Tendilla E 25 D2
Tenebrón E 22 C4
Terradillos de los Templarios E 13 D3
Terrassa E 28 C2
Terrasson-la-Villedieu F 9 E4
Teruel E 26 B1
Teulada E 43 E4
Thenon F 9 E4
Thuir F 18 B1
Tinajo E 43 d2
Tineo E 4 B3

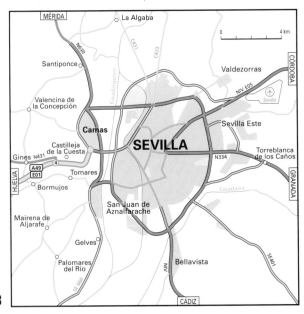

Tirgo E 14 C3
Tobarra E 35 E1
Tocha P 10 A1
Toledo E 24 A1
Tolosa E 15 E4
Tomar P 21 D3
Tomelloso E 34 C3
Tona E 28 C3
Tondela P 10 C1
Tonneins F 8 C3
Tordera E 29 D3
Tordesillas E 13 D2
Toreno E 3 F1
Torija E 25 D3
Torla E 16 B2
Toro E 12 C2
Torrão P 30 C4
Torre E 40 A2
Torre Baja E 36 B4
Torre de la Higuera E 38 B4
Torre de Moncorvo P 11 E2
Torre del Bierzo E 4 A2
Torre del Mar E 40 A2
Torre Vä P 30 C3
Torreblanca E 37 D4
Torredembarra E 28 A2
Torredonjimeno E 40 B4
Torregamones E 12 B2
Torrejón de la Calzada E 24 B2
Torrejón el Rubio E 22 C2
Torrelaguna E 24 C3
Torrelapaja E 25 F4
Torrelavega E 5 F2
Torrelodones E 24 B3
Torremolinos E 39 F2
Torrenostra E 37 D4
Torrente de Cinca E 27 E3
Torrenueva E 40 B1
Torrequemada E 22 B1
Torres Novas P 21 D3
Torres Vedras P 20 B2
Torrevieja E 42 C3
Torrijos E 24 A2
Torroella de Montgri E 29 E3
Tortosa E 27 E1
Tossa de Mar E 29 D3
Totana E 42 A3
Toulouse F 17 F3
Tournay F 16 C3
Tournon-d'Agenais F 9 D3
Trabadelo E 3 E1
Tragacete E 25 F1
Trancoso P 11 D1
Trebujena E 38 C3
Tremp E 28 A4
Trie F 17 D3
Trindade P 11 E2
Tróia P 20 B1
Trujillo E 22 C1
Tubilla de Agua E 14 A4
Tuchan F 18 B2
Tudela E 15 E1
Tudela de Duero E 13 D2
Tui E 2 B1
Tuineje E 43 d1
Tulle F 9 F4
Turégano E 24 B4
Turre E 41 F2

Úbeda E 40 C4
Ugijar E 40 C2
Ulldecona E 27 E1

Ulldemolins E 27 F2
Unquera E 5 E3
Urdos F 16 B3
Usagre E 32 B3
Ustaritz F 7 E1
Utiel E 36 A3
Utrera E 38 C3
Uzès F 19 F3

Vagos P 10 B2
Valcarlos E 15 F3
Valdeltormo E 27 D2
Valdemorillo E 24 B3
Valdenoceda E 14 B4
Valdepeñas E 34 B2
Valdoviño E 3 D4
Vale de Açor P 31 D2
Vale de Cambra P 10 C2
Vale do Lobo P 30 C1
Valença do Minho P 2 B1
Valence F 8 C2
Valence F 9 D2
Valence d'Albigeois F 18 B4
Valencia E 36 C2
Valencia de Alcántara E 21 F2
Valencia de Don Juan E 12 C3
Valencia de las Torres E 32 B3
Vall de Uxó E 36 C3
Vallado E 4 A3
Valladolid E 13 D2
Valldemosa E 44 C4
Valle de loc Caidos E 24 B3
Vallehermoso E 42 a1
Valleraugue F 19 D4
Vallivana E 27 D1
Vallon-Pont-d'Arc F 19 F4
Valls E 28 A2
Valpaços P 11 E3
Valras-Plage F 18 C2
Valtierra E 15 E2
Valverde E 42 a1
Valverde del Camino E 31 F1
Valverde del Fresno E 22 B3
Vandellós E 27 E2
Varilhes F 17 F2
Vauvert F 19 E3
Vayrac F 9 F4
Vecinos E 23 D4
Vegadeo E 3 F3
Vejer de la Frontera E 38 B2
Vélez Blanco E 41 F3
Vélez Rubio E 41 F3
Vélez-Málaga E 40 A2
Venda de Galizes P 21 E4
Venda Nova P 11 D3
Vendargues F 19 E3
Vendas Novas P 20 C1
Venta de Arraco E 16 A3
Venta de Cardeña E 33 E2
Vera E 41 F2
Vera de Bidasoa E 7 D1
Verfeil F 17 F3
Vergt F 9 D4
Verin E 11 E4
Vernet F 17 E3
Vernet-les-Bains F 18 A1
Vézénobres F 19 E4
Viana do Alentejo P 31 D4
Viana do Bolo E 11 F4
Viana do Castelo P 10 B4
Vianne F 8 C2

Vias F 19 D2
Vic E 28 C3
Vic-en-Bigorre F 16 C3
Vic-Fezensac F 8 C2
Vicdessos F 17 E2
Vidigueira P 31 D3
Viella E 17 D2
Vieux-Boucau-les-Bains F 7 E2
Vigo E 2 B1
Vila de Rei P 21 D3
Vila do Bispo P 30 A2
Vila do Conde P 10 B3
Vila Flor P 11 E2
Vila Franca de Xira P 20 B2
Vila Fresca de Azeitão P 20 B1
Vila Nova da Cerveira P 2 B1
Vila Nova de Famaliçao P 10 C3
Vila Nova de Foz Côa P 11 E2
Vila Nova de Milfontes P 30 B3
Vila Nova de Ourém P 21 D3
Vila Nova de Paiva P 11 D2
Vila Pouca de Aguiar P 11 D3
Vila Praia de Âncora P 10 C4
Vila Real P 11 D3
Vila Real de Santo António P 31 D1
Vila Velha de Ródão P 21 E3
Vila Verde de Ficalho P 31 E2
Vila Viçosa P 31 E4
Vila-rodona E 28 A2
Viladamat E 29 E3
Vilafranca del Penedés E 28 B2
Vilagarcía de Arousa E 2 B2
Vilamoura P 30 C1
Vilanova de Arousa E 2 B2
Vilanova i la Geltrú E 28 B2
Vilar Formoso P 22 B4
Vilassar de Mar E 28 C2
Villa Fruela E 13 F2
Villablino E 4 B3
Villacañas E 34 C4
Villacarlos E 45 F3
Villacarrillo E 41 D4
Villacastín E 24 A3
Villada E 13 D3
Villadiego E 13 F3
Villafranca de los Barros E 32 B3
Villafranca del Bierzo E 3 E1
Villafranca del Cid E 26 C1
Villafranca Montes de Oca E 14 B3
Villahermosa E 34 C2
Villahoz E 13 F2
Villajoyosa E 43 D4
Villalba E 3 D3
Villalba E 24 B3
Villalba de la Sierra E 25 E1
Villalcázar de Sirga E 13 E3
Villalón de Campos E 13 D3
Villalpando E 12 C3
Villamañán E 12 C4
Villamanín E 4 C2
Villamartín de Campos E 13 E3
Villandraut F 8 B3
Villanueva de Argaño E 13 F3
Villanueva de Córdoba E 33 E2
Villanueva de Gallego E 26 C4
Villanueva de la Serena E 32 C4
Villanueva de la Sierra E 22 C3
Villanueva de la Vera E 23 D2
Villanueva de los Castillejos E 31 E1
Villanueva de los Infantes E 34 C2
Villanueva del Arzobispo E 41 D4
Villanueva del Campo E 12 C3
Villanueva del Fresno E 31 E3
Villanueva del Huerva E 26 B3
Villarcayo E 6 A1
Villardefrades E 12 C2

X

Y

Z